Insights into Digital Literacy in Language Teaching

Insights into Digital Literacy in Language Teaching explores digital literacy, digital pedagogies, digital technologies, and digital language teaching. The book responds to the need for language teachers to develop and improve digital competencies and digital language teaching strategies. It highlights five key elements of digital literacy: information search and evaluation; creation; communication; collaboration; and online safety. It provides a theoretical basis and a practical guide for language teachers and researchers with any degree of experience in technology-enhanced language teaching. It is a valuable resource for pre-service and in-service language teachers, teacher educators, and researchers.

Jeong-Bae Son is Professor of Applied Linguistics and TESOL in the School of Education at the University of Southern Queensland, Australia. His areas of specialisation are computer-assisted language learning and language teacher education. He serves as the President of the Asia-Pacific Association for Computer-Assisted Language Learning.

Language Teaching Insights Series

Series Editors: David Nunan & Glenn Stockwell

Burston & Arispe: *Mobile-Assisted Language Learning and Advanced-level Second Language Acquisition*

Eginli: *Insights into Emotional Well-Being of Language Teachers*

Farrell: *Insights into Professional Development in Language Teaching*

Horwitz: *Becoming a Language Teacher (2nd ed.)*

Jitpaisarnwattana & Reinders: *Insights into Language MOOCs*

Khezrlou: *Insights into Task-Based Language Teaching*

Lai: *Insights into Autonomy and Technology in Language Teaching*

Leis: *Insights into Flipped Classrooms*

Mohebbi (Ed.): *Insights into Teaching and Learning Writing*

Son: *Insights into Digital Literacy in Language Teaching*

Tanaka-Ellis: *Insights into Teaching and Learning with Technology*

More information about titles in this series can be found at
https://www.castledown.com/academic-books/book-series/language-teaching-insights/

Insights into Digital Literacy in Language Teaching

Jeong-Bae Son

Melbourne – London – Tokyo – New York

4th Floor, Silverstream House, 45 Fitzroy Street Fitzrovia, London W1T 6EB, United Kingdom
Level 9, 440 Collins Street, Melbourne, Victoria 3000, Australia
2nd Floor Daiya Building, 2-2-15 Hamamatsu-cho, Minato-ku, Tokyo 105-0013, Japan
447 Broadway, 2nd Floor #393, New York NY, 10013, United States

First published 2024 by Castledown Publishers, London

Information on this title:
www.castledown.com/academic-books/view-title/?reference=9781914291210

DOI: 10.29140/9781914291210

Insights into Digital Literacy in Language Teaching

© Jeong-Bae Son, 2024

All rights reserved. This publication is copyright. Subject to statutory exception and to the provisions of relevant collective licencing agreements, no reproduction, transmission, or storage of any part of this publication by any means, electronic, mechanical, photocopying, recording or otherwise may take place without prior written permission from the author.

Typeset by Chennai Publishing Services Pvt. Ltd.
ISBN: 978-1-914291-21-0

Castledown Publishers takes no responsibility for the accuracy of URLs for external or third-party internet websites referred to in this publication. No responsibility is taken for the accuracy or appro-priateness of information found in any of these websites.

Table of Contents

List of Tables — vi
List of Figures — vii
Acknowledgements — viii
Abbreviations — ix
Preface — xi

Chapter 1. Digital Literacy and Language Teaching — 1

    1.1 Understanding digital literacy — 1
    1.2 Impacts and contributions — 8
    1.3 Challenges and issues — 14

Chapter 2. Information Search and Evaluation — 19

    2.1 Searching for information — 19
    2.2 Evaluating information — 24
    2.3 Developing information search and evaluation skills — 27

Chapter 3. Creation — 34

    3.1 Creating content — 34
    3.2 Developing digital content creation skills — 38

Chapter 4. Communication — 51

    4.1 Communicating online — 51
    4.2 Developing digital communication skills — 55

Chapter 5. Collaboration — 68

    5.1 Collaborating online — 68
    5.2 Developing digital collaboration skills — 74

Chapter 6. Online Safety — 87

    6.1 Being safe online — 87
    6.2 Developing online safety skills — 92

Chapter 7. Digital Language Teaching — 103

    7.1 Digital literacy education and language teaching — 104
    7.2 Digital pedagogies and digital technologies — 111
    7.3 Developing digital language teaching skills — 131

References — 145

Index — 161

List of Tables

Table 1.1 Elements of Digital Literacy in Previous Studies (adapted from Son et al., 2017, p. 79) — 6

Table 3.1 Roles of Multiple Intelligence in Digital Content Creation (adapted from Ivers & Barron, 2015, p. 8) — 36

Table 5.1 Collaborative Language Learning Technologies (adapted from Su & Zou, 2022, pp. 1787–1788) — 72

Table 7.1 Principles and Pedagogical Goals of a Relational Pedagogy (adapted from Kern, 2015, p. 223) — 113

Table 7.2 Dimensions of Digital Literacies and Example Practices (adapted from Hafner et al., 2015, pp. 2–3) — 116

Table 7.3 Online Tools for Language Teaching (adapted from Son, 2023c) — 118

Table 7.4 Digital Tools Suggested for Five Key Elements of Digital Literacy — 123

Table 7.5 Example Digital Literacy Planner — 126

Table 7.6 Online Activities for Language Learning (adapted from Son, 2023d) — 127

Table 7.7 Digital Language Teacher Development Framework (DLTDF) (Son, 2020b, pp. 7–8) — 136

Table 7.8 Competency Levels of the Digital Language Teacher Development Framework (Son, 2020b, pp. 8–9) — 138

List of Figures

Figure 1.1 Elements of Digital Literacy (Son, 2015)   7
Figure 7.1 Bases of Digital Language Teaching   103
Figure 7.2 Categories of Online Tools for Language
    Teaching (Son, 2010)   117

Acknowledgements

I am grateful for all teachers, students, and researchers I have worked with in digital environments. It has been amazing to explore and interact with them. I would also like to thank colleagues and collaborators who have made contributions to my research projects in various ways. It has been great to communicate and collaborate with them. In addition, I want to thank readers of this book. We can learn from each other and connect with potential readers. Finally yet importantly, my special thanks go to my family for their love and support. It is a wonderful journey with them. Thank you, everyone!

Abbreviations

ACMC	Asynchronous Computer-Mediated Communication
AI	Artificial Intelligence
APACALL	Asia-Pacific Association for Computer-Assisted Language Learning
AR	Augmented Reality
ASR	Automatic Speech Recognition
AWE	Automated Writing Evaluation
CALL	Computer-Assisted Language Learning
CAT	Computer Adaptive Testing
CDA	Computerized Dynamic Assessment
CMC	Computer-Mediated communication
CPD	Continuing Professional Development
DDL	Data-Driven Learning
DLTDF	Digital Language Teacher Development Framework
EAP	English for Academic Purposes
ECCR	Exploration – Communication – Collaboration – Reflection
EFL	English as a Foreign Language
ESL	English as a Second Language
FL	Foreign Language
GPT	Generative Pre-trained Transformer
ICALL	Intelligent Computer-Assisted Language Learning
ICC	Intercultural communicative competence
ICT	Information and Communication Technology
IPA	Intelligent Personal Assistant
ITS	Intelligent Tutoring System
L2	Second Language
LMS	Learning Management System
MALL	Mobile-Assisted Language Learning
MT	Machine Translation
NLP	Natural Language Processing
OER	Open Educational Resource
SCMC	Synchronous Computer-Mediated Communication
SMS	Short Message Service
SNS	Social Networking Service

TELT	Technology-Enhanced Language Teaching
TESOL	Teaching English to Speakers of Other Languages
TPACK	Technological Pedagogical and Content Knowledge
VR	Virtual Reality

Preface

We live and work in the digital world and use digital devices and tools for various purposes, whether like it or not. The effective use of digital technologies for education has been a key issue for many educators and researchers. In language education, there is an ongoing need for language teachers to develop and improve digital literacy skills and digital language teaching strategies. The need continuously raises the questions of what language teachers should know about digital literacy, what knowledge and skills are required for using digital technologies in language teaching, and how teachers can implement digital language teaching effectively. This book responds to these questions in a strategic way. The book is intended to provide a theoretical basis and a practical guide for language teachers and researchers with any degree of experience in technology-enhanced language teaching.

The book consists of seven chapters and examines digital literacy, digital tools, and digital language teaching. Chapter 1 introduces the concepts of digital literacy, outlines the impacts and contributions of digital literacy, and discusses challenges and issues with digital literacy. Chapter 2 deals with main aspects of searching for and evaluating information and explores ways of developing information search and evaluation skills. Chapter 3 delves into creating digital content and explores ways of developing digital content creation skills. Chapter 4 focuses on digital communication and explores ways of developing digital communication skills. Chapter 5 covers digital collaboration and explores ways of developing digital collaboration skills. Chapter 6 explains what the meaning of online safety is and explores ways of developing online safety skills. Finally, Chapter 7 discusses digital literacy education, digital pedagogies, and digital technologies and suggests ways of developing digital language teaching skills.

The book serves as a valuable resource for pre-service and in-service language teachers, teacher educators, and researchers. It offers opportunities for readers to engage in discussions on digital literacy in language teaching, digital tools for language teaching, and digital language teaching. I hope that the book provides meaningful insights into digital literacy in language teaching for further research and practice.

Jeong-Bae Son
November 2023

1
Digital Literacy and Language Teaching

Digital literacy is essential for individuals in today's digital world. It is critical for language learners to be digitally literate in digital environments where digital technologies are used for language learning. It is also crucial for language teachers to develop their digital literacy skills and strategies while using digital tools and resources for language teaching. This chapter looks into the interrelationship between digital literacy and language teaching. It consists of three sections: (1) understanding digital literacy; (2) impacts and contributions; and (3) challenges and issues. Tasks in each section of this chapter are presented in line with Son's (2018) exploration-communication-collaboration-reflection (ECCR) model.

1.1 Understanding digital literacy

We start with the concepts of digital literacy, which have evolved along with the rapid advancement of digital technologies. Many researchers and practitioners have defined digital literacy. In the late 1990s, Gilster (1997) defined digital literacy as "the ability to understand and use information in multiple formats from a wide range of sources when it is presented via computers" (p. 1). Later, Martin (2005) proposed that digital literacy is "the awareness, attitude and ability of individuals to appropriately use digital tools and facilities to identify, access, manage, integrate, evaluate, analyse and synthesize digital resources, construct new knowledge, create media expressions, and communicate with others, in the context of specific life situations, in order to enable constructive social action; and to reflect upon this process" (pp. 135–136). In a similar vein, Hague and Payton (2010) stated that digital literacy is "the ability to make and share meaning in different modes and formats; to create, collaborate and communicate effectively and to understand how and when digital technologies can best be used to support these processes" (p. 2).

Hobbs (2010) used the term "digital and media literacy" and defined it as "a constellation of life skills that are necessary for full participation in our media-saturated, information-rich society" (p. vii). She included the following abilities in digital and media literacy:

- Make responsible choices and access information by locating and sharing materials and comprehending information and ideas
- Analyze messages in a variety of forms by identifying the author, purpose and point of view, and evaluating the quality and credibility of the content
- Create content in a variety of forms, making use of language, images, sound, and new digital tools and technologies
- Reflect on one's own conduct and communication behavior by applying social responsibility and ethical principles
- Take social action by working individually and collaboratively to share knowledge and solve problems in the family, workplace and community, and by participating as a member of a community   (pp. vii–viii)

Ng (2012) considered digital literacy as "the multiplicity of literacies associated with the use of digital technologies" and said, "These technologies are a subset of electronic technologies that include hardware and software used by individuals for educational, social and/or entertainment purposes in schools and at home" (p. 1066). Meyers et al. (2013) suggested an expanded view of digital literacy, which "accounts for an expanded understanding of a digitally literate person as a creative agent who operates within a socio-technical network that affords opportunities for extension, sharing and learning" (p. 363). They highlighted the importance of informal learning in informal contexts such as the home, libraries, museums, and online spaces and stated, "The environment in which this form of digital literacy comes into play most fully is the informal environment in which these agents can express themselves most fully outside the bounds and constraints of a curricular agenda and standards" (p. 363). In a book on mobile-assisted language learning (MALL), Stockwell (2022) pointed out that the term digital literacy has evolved to include "a range of individual skills and related literacies such as information literacy (the ability to seek and organise information) (Weibe, 2016), multimodal literacy (the ability to deal with information that comes through multiple modes) (Lotherington & Jenson, 2011), and media literacy (the ability to evaluate the credibility of sources and to create new messages based on the information taken from these sources) (Buckingham, 2007)" (p. 57).

Ferrari (2012) used the term "digital competence" and explained digital competence as "the set of knowledge, skills, attitudes (thus including abilities, strategies, values and awareness) that are required when using ICT and digital media to perform tasks; solve problems; communicate; manage information; collaborate; create and share content; and build knowledge effectively, efficiently, appropriately, critically, creatively, autonomously, flexibly, ethically, reflectively for work, leisure, participation, learning, socialising, consuming, and empowerment" (p. 43). In a study of experts' views on digital competence, Janssen et al. (2013) reported that digital competence was seen as "a conglomerate of knowledge, skills, and attitudes connected to various purposes (communication, creative expression, information management, personal development, etc.), domains (daily life, work, privacy & security, legal aspects), and levels" (p. 479). They stated, "Digital competence clearly involves more than knowing how to use devices and applications – which is intricately connected with skills to communicate using ICT as well as information management skills. Besides, sensible and healthy use of ICT requires particular knowledge and attitudes regarding legal and ethical aspects, privacy and security, as well as an understanding of the role of ICT in society and a balanced attitude towards technology" (p. 480). They also commented that "digital competence requires the ability to learn about and with digital technologies, to choose the right technology and to do so in confidence" (p. 480).

On the other hand, Jisc (n.d.), which is a UK not-for-profit company supporting higher education, uses the term "digital capability" to explain "the skills and attitudes that individuals and organisations need if they are to thrive in today's world" and defines individual digital capabilities as "those which equip someone to live, learn and work in a digital society" (para. 1). Its digital capabilities framework consists of six elements: digital proficiency and productivity (functional skills); information, data, and media literacies (critical use); digital creation, problem solving, and innovation (creative production); digital communication, collaboration, and participation (participation); digital learning and development (development); and digital identity and wellbeing (self-actualising). It also provides a series of role profiles for different groups of individuals such as teachers, students, and researchers and shows an interest in digital wellbeing, which is impacted by digital technologies and services.

Through a systematic literature review, van Laar et al. (2017) examined the relationship between 21st century skills and digital skills and pointed out that 21st century skills are broader than digital skills. In association with information and communication technologies (ICTs) use, they introduced 21st century digital skills and identified seven core skills: technical skills ("to use (mobile) devices and applications to accomplish practical tasks and recognize specific online environments to navigate and maintain orientation"); information management skills ("to use ICT to efficiently search, select, organize information to make informed decisions about the most suitable sources of information for a given task"); communication skills ("to use ICT to transmit information to others, ensuring that the meaning is expressed effectively"); collaboration skills ("to use ICT to develop a social network and work in a team to exchange information, negotiate agreements, and make decisions with mutual respect for each other towards achieving a common goal"); creativity skills ("to use ICT to generate new or previously unknown ideas, or treat familiar ideas in a new way and transform such ideas into a product, service or process that is recognized as novel within a particular domain"); critical thinking skills ("to use ICT to make informed judgements and choices about obtained information and communication using effective reasoning and sufficient evidence to support the claims"); and problem-solving skills ("to use ICT to cognitively process and understand a problem situation in combination with the active use of knowledge to find a solution to a problem") (p. 583). They also identified five contextual 21st century digital skills: ethical awareness skills ("to behave in a socially responsible way, demonstrating awareness and knowledge of legal and ethical aspects when using ICT"); cultural awareness skills ("to show cultural understanding and respect other cultures when using ICT"); flexibility skills ("to adapt one's thinking, attitude or behavior to changing ICT environments"); self-direction skills ("to set goals for yourself and manage progression toward reaching those goals in order to assess your own progress when using ICT"); and lifelong learning skills ("to constantly explore new opportunities when using ICT that can be integrated into an environment to continually improve one's capabilities") (p. 583). Dreamson (2020) also looked at the relationship between digital literacy and 21st centruy skills and highlighted digital literacy as a set of 21st century skills, including critical thinking, communication, collaboration, and creativity. He supported the idea that these skills are important for global citizenship education and argued that there is a need for meta-ethical understanding of the skills.

Digital literacy is often pluralised as digital literacies to reflect different forms, functions, and types of literacy practices in different contexts (Dudeney et al., 2013; Kern, 2021; Lankshear & Knobel, 2008; Thorne, 2013; Ware et al., 2016). Dudeney et al. (2013) considered digital literacies as "the individual and social skills needed to effectively interpret, manage, share and create meaning in the growing range of digital communication channels" (p. 2). See Pegrum (2023) for an additional list of specific types of digital literacies, including hypertext literacy, multimodal literacy, mobile literacy, information literacy, intercultural literacy, and critical literacy. Similarly, Jisc (2014) stated, "Digital literacies are those capabilities which fit an individual for living, learning and working in a digital society" (para. 1). Guikema and Williams (2014) asserted that "digital literacies are conceptualized as a way of being an engaged, responsible, reflective citizen in a 21st century global community permeated by multimodal technologies" (p. 3) while Jones and Hafner (2021) noted that digital literacies are "the practices of communicating, relating, thinking and 'being' associated with digital media" (p. 13). Related to language learning, Kern (2021) added, "Digital literacies integrate listening, speaking, viewing, reading, writing, and critical thinking, along with the skills necessary to operate digital devices and navigate their various resources" (p. 143). Digital literacies are digitally mediated multimodal literacies (Lotherington & Jenson, 2011). They need to be conceptualised within a specific context (Bilki et al., 2023).

In this book, digital literacy is defined as "the ability to use digital technologies at an adequate level for creation, communication, collaboration, and information search and evaluation in a digital society. It involves the development of knowledge and skills for using digital devices and tools for specific purposes" (Son, 2015, para. 1). It can also involve experiencing and thinking about the reality (Hafner et al., 2015) and social issues raised by the use of digital technologies (Chen, 2020). The term *digital literacies* are used where there is a need to indicate different knowledge, skills, and practices of digital literacy. As indicated in its definition, digital literacy entails a range of elements. Son et al. (2017) provided a summary of elements of digital literacy proposed and discussed in several publications (see Table 1.1). The elements listed in each publication have both similarities and differences and reflect general and distinctive features and focuses. Among them, Son's (2015) five elements (i.e., information search and evaluation; creation; communication; collaboration; and online safety (ICCCO)) are the key elements that are highlighted and extensively discussed in this book. Thus, the summary below (illustrated in Figure 1.1) is explained and expanded throughout the book:

- Information search and evaluation – Find, evaluate, and manage information
- Creation – Create meaning, activities, materials, and resources
- Communication – Communicate in digital networks effectively
- Collaboration – Work with others while sharing ideas and resources
- Online safety – Develop critical engagement and safe practices

Table 1.1 *Elements of Digital Literacy in Previous Studies (adapted from Son et al., 2017, p. 79)*

Eshet-Alkalai (2004)	[Types of digital literacy] • Photo-visual literacy • Reproduction literacy • Branching literacy • Information literacy • Socio-emotional literacy
Calvani et al. (2008)	[Dimensions of digital competence] • Technological dimension • Cognitive dimension • Ethical dimension • Integration between the three dimensions
Hague & Payton (2010)	[Components of digital literacy] • Functional skills • E-safety • Effective communication • The ability to find and select information • Collaboration • Cultural and social understanding • Critical thinking and evaluation • Creativity
Ferrari (2013)	[Areas of digital competence] • Information • Communication • Content creation • Safety • Problem solving
Belshaw (2014)	[Elements of digital literacies] • Cultural element • Cognitive element • Constructive element • Communicative element • Confident element • Creative element • Critical element • Civic element

Continued....

Table 1.1 *Continued....*

Jisc (2014)	[Elements of digital literacies] • Media literacy • Communications and collaboration • Career & identity management • ICT literacy • Learning skills • Digital scholarship • Information literacy
Son (2015)	[Elements of digital literacy] • Information search and evaluation • Creation • Communication • Collaboration • Online safety

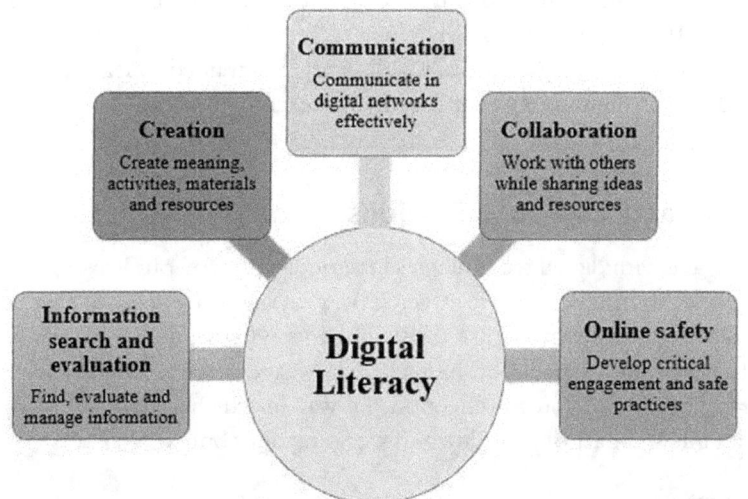

Figure 1.1 *Elements of Digital Literacy (Son, 2015)*

Task 1.1

Exploration

Google for Education (https://edu.google.com/) provides a range of videos for teachers and students to learn about practical digital skills. Explore its Applied Digital Skills site (https://applieddigitalskills.withgoogle.com/).

Choose a video from the site and discuss how the video can be used in your language classroom.

Communication

Digital literacy includes the ability to engage in online communication. Which digital technology or tool do you use most frequently for digitally mediated communication? Explain why and how you use it.

Collaboration

Participate in a group discussion on different elements of digital literacy and present a summary of the group discussion.

Reflection

Recall your past or current training in digital literacy and answer the questions below:

- Has the training helped you have a clear understanding of digital literacy? If yes, how? If no, why not?
- What types of digital literacy skills were you trained to learn and use?
- How has the training influenced your teaching practice?

1.2 Impacts and contributions

We engage with digital technologies in various facets of our lives. Our daily activities and interactions are affected by what digital devices we have, how we use them, and why we use them. The following vignettes are examples that show some aspects of individual language teachers' digital life and work. They invite you to reflect on the way in which digital technologies are an integral part of your life and work in your context.

Vignette 1

I use several digital devices in my daily life. The digital devices I regularly use include an iMac, a MacBook Pro, an iPad Air (3rd generation), and an iPhone SE. I use all of these in both my professional career and personal life. Although I predominantly teach in classroom settings, my classes are all paperless. My students have computer access during class time, so course materials are available online. I mainly use my iMac and MacBook Pro for curriculum design, lesson planning, research, data collection and analysis, article writing, and presentations. Rather than using textbooks, I prefer to create authentic teaching materials. To do this, I spend considerable time scouring the internet, looking for interesting content. Recently, I have been experimenting with ChatGPT to help edit texts and create comprehension questions for reading and listening tasks. The lesson materials I make, I upload to the open-source learning platform moodle.org, which my students can access both inside and outside the classroom. I like the web-based presentation tool prezi.com for both in-class and conference presentations. It is easy to use, looks professional, and allows me to add links to Moodle. I also can make recordings, which my students can then go back and listen to in their own time. To relax in my free time, I mainly use my iPad to keep up with the news, read books on Kindle, watch documentaries on Netflix, Amazon Prime, or YouTube, and occasionally play online games. I find I only use my iPhone to sometimes have Zoom meetings, make actual telephone calls, or use Google Maps to help me get from A to B. As the digital devices I own encompass almost every aspect of my life, I find the line between work and home can sometimes become blurred. That is why I occasionally feel the need to step away.

Anthony Young

Reflection

- What can you learn from writing about how you manage the use of digital devices in your context?
- How often do you think you need to have digital-free time?

Vignette 2

I start my mornings quickly checking my phone, perhaps scrolling content on a social media page for about 10 minutes more than I should. Justifying this process as entertainment, like a quick look at the morning newspaper, keeping me connected to friends and family around the world. I view my phone as a tool for my benefit, as opposed to a tool for everyone else's endless access to me. I have the right to not read a text for two hours. Nevertheless, I am usually always available unless I am using my phone to stream a Netflix or Disney documentary through my headsets while I renovate my house. Listening to the stories of others, fascinated by their realities while conducting repetitive painting strokes! For entertainment, I have both the PlayStation VR and Oculus Rift. The only downside of my use of these tools is that my brain still has issues with visual movement not corresponding with physical movement, resulting in feelings of nausea. I am able to reduce this effect by mimicking the movement in VR with my body, but in fast visual moving games where I am running in VR, I still have issues with the length of play time. It is probably a blessing in disguise as it reduces my gaming time. I am very interested in researching in VR. I do not watch television but watch a selected movie or episode of a series, streamed through my laptop and projector onto a projector screen relaxing in my jacuzzi after working out, relaxing my muscles and my mind. When driving, I use Siri, Apple's digital assistance, to select songs to listen to using voice commands. This allows me to interact with media while concentrating on driving. At present, I listen to an application for learning Italian while in the car. In my work at a research institute, my laptop is everything. It provides me online access to the latest concepts and research in my focus fields. I use it to read, write and collaborate. While teaching at university, I complement my face-to-face teaching with the use of a learning management system, where digital methods are used to share documents and ideas on group forums. I also mark student essays digitally allowing me to add comments to sections. In class, I use a PC and a projector to show relevant videos and information. And this is the aspect that often has a negative impact, before going to sleep I often continue watching a Netflix series. Weekly I tell myself, "you must learn to go to sleep before midnight", but actually thinking sleep is a boring waste of time yet an action I cannot avoid. My phone enables my bad behaviour as I watch one episode and maybe just one more until 1 or 2am. I awake at 6.30am and curse my bad behaviour, then usually repeat. I must learn to limit myself to one episode, but it is so difficult if it happens to be a good series. The readily available content is a blessing and a curse. I love my digital opportunities and downfalls!

Natasha Ružić

Reflection

- What kinds of self-directed professional development activities have you found most useful?
- What do you think could be done for managing screen time?

Vignette 3

I use digital devices extensively in my daily and professional life. Over the years, I have found that the important aspects of my life such as teaching (e.g., storage and retrieval of materials), researching (e.g., searching journals), personal fitness (e.g., fitness tracking), and personal relationships (e.g., instant messaging) benefit greatly from being in their digital forms rather than their traditional forms. Therefore, I embrace new technology and welcome it into my life when it provides value. My PC at home is the central point for work to get done. I spend my time on my home computer researching literature and planning lessons. Having three monitors and a fast internet connection allows me to work effectively and efficiently. Software packages that are essential to my work and research include Microsoft Office, Google Workspace, and Adobe Creative Cloud. When I am away from the home office, I use a MacBook. I find MacBook laptops to be more reliable than PC laptops. Reliability is essential when you are a teacher that uses a computer in class. As an EFL teacher, choosing suitable textbooks is an important part of the job. Many textbooks these days come with digital presentation tools. These tools allow for textbooks to be easily displayed on a class projector. They also include all listening materials and answers. Digital presentation tools make it easy for the teacher and students to follow along with and are now an essential component to consider when I choose a textbook. If I am away from my PC or MacBook, I use my iPhone for a range of tasks (e.g., looking up information, playing media, social media). I use an Apple Watch in class to track time; specifically, if students are doing a timed activity, it is very easy to start a stopwatch on my Apple Watch. For teaching, my future goal is to move students' handouts away from paper to digital forms. This is mostly due to the negative environmental impact of using too much paper.

Andrew Philpott

Reflection

- What do you think are the characteristics of effective digital teaching?
- What would you include in a list of digital devices/tools that would be useful for your research or teaching?

Along with the integration of digital technologies into the language classroom (Bui, 2022; Carrier et al., 2017; Galla, 2016; Son, 2020a, 2023a; Zou et al., 2021), digital literacy has significantly influenced language education and plays a critical role in language learning and teaching (Carillo, 2022; Oskoz & Elola, 2020; Reinhardt & Thorne, 2019; Stockwell, 2015). In a study of the role of digital literacy in student engagement with automated writing evaluation (AWE) feedback in a general English course at a Chinese university, for example, Zhang and Hyland (2023) found that the students' digital literacy had a considerable impact on how they engaged with AWE feedback, regardless of their language proficiency. They highlighted that students' digital literacy is a key factor in effective student engagement with AWE feedback on L2 writing.

Digital literacy allows language teachers to implement blended learning approaches, which combine in-person learning and online learning and facilitate personalised learning activities (e.g., Andujar & Nadif, 2022; Li, 2022; Mizza & Rubio, 2020; Sato et al., 2020). It also allows language teachers to enhance their students' language learning experiences by using a wide range of digital tools and resources, including computer-mediated communication (CMC) tools, mobile apps, online dictionaries, grammar guides, online courses, language learning websites, educational games, images, audios, and videos (see Son, 2023c, for a list of example digital tools and Son, 2016, for a list of example mobile apps).

In addition, digital literacy allows language teachers to create virtual language exchange activities for themselves and their students, which promote intercultural understanding, collaboration, and interaction (e.g., Canals, 2020; Lenkaitis, 2022; O'Dowd & Dooly, 2022; O'Dowd & O'Rourke, 2019). In a study of the benefits of participating in a virtual exchange for practicing oral skills, Canals (2020) concluded that virtual exchanges offer "a unique space for one-on-one intensive language practice with native speakers, which neatly complements the activities conducted in regular (online) courses, where access to native speakers is usually restricted to the teacher and other language input, such as course materials" (p. 114). Furthermore, digital literacy can open up flexible learning opportunities for language learners and teachers in virtual learning environments (e.g., Comas-Quinn et al., 2012; Jin et al., 2022; Manegre & Sabiri, 2022). Jin et al. (2022), for instance, investigated their participants' engagement in asynchronous online discussions in a computer-assisted language learning (CALL) course and reported that engagement patterns were observed in discussion posts and a high level of cognitive engagement was achieved through the presence of social mediators.

Kern (2021) discussed major contributions of digital literacies to language learning in terms of three themes: agency, autonomy, and identity; creativity; and new sociality and communities. He pointed out that digital literacies offered language learners new opportunities to develop agency and autonomy, express their identities (through social media, telecollaborative exchanges, forums, and other platforms), and showcase their creativity (through multimodal composition, fan fiction, games, and other contacts). He also mentioned that new forms of sociality have been developed in digital environments and the interactive and social nature of digital literacies are emphasised in social learning contexts such as online games, virtual exchange, and digital social reading. He underlined that participation in online communities requires "well developed digital literacy that includes intercultural sensibilities and openness to new perspectives" (p. 140). This implies that a high level of digital literacy with an intercultural understanding and open mind allows language learners to participate in online communities meaningfully and constructively.

Task 1.2

Exploration
Are you active in exploring digital tools and resources for language learning and teaching? If yes, why? If no, why not? Respond and discuss.

Communication
How do you think digital literacy has affected the way we communicate? Respond and discuss.

Collaboration
How do you think digital literacy can contribute to collaborative language learning and teaching? Respond and discuss.

Reflection
What impacts do you think digital literacy have on language learning and teaching? Reflect on your experience.

1.3 Challenges and issues

In relation to digital literacy, there are challenges and issues that need to be addressed. One of the challenges is a digital divide. Concerns about the digital divide include the unequal access to and use of digital technologies (Ragnedda & Muschert, 2013) and people's different levels of skills to use digital devices, information, and resources (Hargittai, 2002; Tate & Warschauer, 2017). McLay and Reyes (2019) pointed out that "the evolving use of the term *digital divide* reflects increasingly nuanced understandings of technology-related equity issues" (p. 19). The digital divide is considered as a social justice issue (Adelore & Ojedeji, 2022). The Centre for Social Justice (2017) based in the UK recognised digital exclusion and stated, "The ever-growing centrality of digital skills and knowledge to everyday life means that to be digitally excluded will often mean a person is socially and economically excluded, leaving them unable to fulfil their potential, find meaningful work and a full education" (p. 8). In the field of CALL, Anwaruddin (2019) discussed the use of social media from a social justice perspective with the idea that teaching for social justice is a democratic act. He proposed a dialogic approach based on serendipity and contingent scaffolding. Lozano and Izquierdo (2019), on the other hand, discussed the potential of teacher education and CALL task implementation to overcome the digital divide and asserted that "material access in the classroom can be overcome through teacher education and task preparation that promote the effective implementation of tasks using the limited technologies that each institution, teacher, and/or student might have" (p. 66).

Kern (2021) considered the following challenges as pedagogical agendas: (1) making learners aware of the importance of digital literacies; (2) the need for more dynamic kinds of assessment; and (3) rethinking the epistemological foundations of L2 writing and how to deal with issues of intellectual property, plagiarism, and fair use. He remarked, "We need to understand the full implications of differential access to electronic literacy tools and the social capital needed to use them effectively" (p. 143). In a survey study measuring three dimensions of digital skills (i.e., theoretical knowledge/awareness; operational skills; and evaluation skills) of high school students, Gui and Argentin (2011) reported that parental education could produce significant differences in the students' possession of digital skills. They found that the students' performance of evaluation skills was poor compared with the other two dimensions and suggested to offer new media literacy interventions for young people. Kurek and Hauck (2014) argued that digital competence requires systematic preparation and training because it is not acquired through simple exposure to digital applications and tools. They presented an instructional model for learner training grounded in multiliteracy and suggested a task-based approach consisting of three components: informed reception, thoughtful participation, and creative contribution. Each component was addressed at the cognitive, social, discursive, and operational levels. In another study on learner training in digital language learning, Son (2019) developed and implemented the training in line with four domains: "technical training (how to use); strategic training (what to do); pedagogical training (why to do); and contextual training (where and when to use)" (p. 30). He added the fourth component (i.e., contextual training) to the first three components adapted from Romeo and Hubbard (2008) to "reflect contextual aspects based on target participants' own experiences, needs and situations" (p. 30).

The next challenge is teacher training and support. Teachers may not feel comfortable and confident in using digital technologies in their teaching if their digital literacy level is low. Teacher training and support programs should be developed and implemented properly as part of teacher development, which is essential for the effective use of digital technologies for language teaching (Son, 2020b). Preparing teachers adequately for language teaching in digital environments has been a key topic in CALL teacher education. Guikema and Menke (2014) investigated foreign language pre-service teachers' views of digital literacies and reported that the teacher candidates expressed a concern about losing control over learning and the technology-enhanced learning environment. They underlined the importance of explicitly addressing digital literacies in teacher training and gave an example approach: "One approach might be to introduce digital literacies in a methods course early on in the term as a way to frame the rest of the experience, followed by regular reflections throughout the term on how digital literacies play out in their instructional practices" (p. 280).

For the implementation of a pedagogy of multiliteracies, Warner and Dupuy (2018) pointed out the need for "models of professional development that emphasize the long-term development of conceptual knowledge and strategies rather than one-off training opportunities" (p. 121) together with textbook materials that adopt a multiliteracies approach. Regarding critical digital literacy development, Bilki et al. (2023) analysed English language teachers' reflections on critical digital literacy as part of their virtual exchange experience and recommended more closely guided and informed reflections on self-representation, inclusiveness, building connections, and social-political landscape.

Another challenge is data security and privacy. Data security is the protection of data. Data privacy is an aspect of data protection against unauthorised access, loss, or corruption (Bigelow, 2022). The increasing use of digital technologies has brought up risks that digital data may be misused, misinterpreted, or abused. Teachers need to have a clear understanding of data privacy and security and implement data protection measures and educate students how to use them. They also need to use digital technologies responsibly and ethically. Marín et al. (2023) explored social media data privacy in education and investigated 225 pre-service teachers' perceptions of the educational use of social media and their awareness and practices of data privacy. They found that the teachers from universities in four countries had concerns about data privacy, but their knowledge about data privacy was lacking. They asserted that teachers need a critical approach to "data literacies, including responsible behavior, copyright, and privacy issues in social media". In a different context, Vartiainen et al. (2022) conducted a study of Finnish pre-service teachers' experiences of data agency in social media environments and reported that the teachers recognised gaps in their knowledge of wider socio-technical systems. They recommended teacher education that broadens teachers' understanding of how data agency is afforded and constrained, how data agency is produced, mediated, augmented, and regulated, and what kinds of implications socio-technical systems have.

There is also an issue of digital distractions, which can negatively impact learning and teaching while using digital devices. Teachers need to develop and implement strategies that increase learner engagement in online learning activities. Göl et al. (2023) investigated Turkish university students' digital distraction levels during the COVID-19 pandemic and reported that digital distractions were negatively related to general satisfaction and perceived learning. They found that the amount of digital distraction, sending instant messages, checking the time, boredom, sharing social media, and system usability were significant predictors of digital distraction. In a different context, Murray et al. (2020) examined undergraduate students' experiences, perceptions, and awareness of distractive technologies in their language learning and performance. They found a lack of student awareness of the final amount of time they spent online but some awareness of the influence of distractive technologies on their language learning. To deal with such distractions, they proposed a critical digital literacy, which they called a strategic deictic agentive literacy.

A recent challenge is the rise of artificial intelligence (AI), particularly AI-powered chatbots such as *ChatGPT* (https://chat.openai.com/). Meniado

(2023) claimed that "AI will be used to provide more personalized language learning opportunities and support in order to help learners achieve their individual learning purpose" and added, "More advanced forms of generative AI for language learning such as the *ChatGPT*, Bard and You.com will likely emerge given the current dynamics of the technology in the market" (p. 9). Son et al. (2023) classified AI technologies and applications for second and foreign language learning and teaching into seven categories: natural language processing (NLP), data-driven learning (DDL), automated writing evaluation (AWE), computerized dynamic assessment (CDA), intelligent tutoring systems (ITSs), automatic speech recognition (ASR), and chatbots. They said, "If carefully planned and used, *ChatGPT* might offer a rich opportunity for language teachers to enhance language teaching" (p. 12). While there are questions about the originality and accuracy of *ChatGPT* responses (e.g., Given, 2023), Kohnke et al. (2023) stated that *ChatGPT* can support "language learning by simulating authentic interactions" (p. 3) and "teachers and students must develop the specific digital competencies needed to use such tools in ways that are pedagogically beneficial and ethical" (p. 10). They suggested three areas of the digital competence teachers need in using *ChatGPT*: technological proficiency; pedagogical compatibility; and social awareness. In addition to these areas, contextual understanding and application might be considered in language teacher development. If language teachers are equipped with AI literacy and design chatbot-supported learning activities thoughtfully, they might utilise AI to offer diverse learning opportunities and engaging learning experiences for language learners.

Task 1.3

Exploration
What challenges do you have in your context? Explore the challenges and suggest strategies to overcome the challenges.

Communication
How do you communicate with others to address digital literacy issues? Share examples of the types of communication you use.

Collaboration
How do you think you can facilitate collaboration among learners of different backgrounds? Respond and make suggestions.

Reflection

Do you consider yourself as a teacher who is competent in dealing with challenges and issues with digital literacy? If yes, how? If no, why not? Reflect on and review your self-monitoring.

Discussion Questions

1. What would you describe what digital literacy is in a sentence?
2. Digital literacy has become a critical aspect of language education in the digital age. What do you think are the roles of digital literacy in language learning and teaching?
3. What kinds of contributions do you think digital literacy can make to language learning and teaching?
4. What knowledge and skills do you think language teachers need in using digital tools and resources for their learning and teaching?
5. How do you think language teachers can help students develop and improve their digital literacy skills?
6. What elements of digital literacy are most important in your context? Why?
7. What do you think about the impact of digital literacy on your teaching?
8. Have you ever experienced any challenge or issue with digital literacy in your teaching? If so, what did you learn from the experience?
9. Is the digital divide an issue in your own context? Why or why not?
10. How do you think you can reduce students' digital distractions in language learning?
11. What benefits do you think teachers can have when they are competent in using digital tools and resources for their teaching?
12. How can we deal with individual, institutional, social, cultural, and contextual differences in digital environments?

2
Information Search and Evaluation

With the rapid development of digital technologies, there have been significant changes to the way we find, access, and use information. The amount of information available online is vast and continuously growing every day. We need to understand how to search for, evaluate, curate, organise, manage, and share information in digital environments (Jones & Hafner, 2021; Mackenzie & Makin, 2003). Searching for and evaluating information is one of the most important skills and practices of digital literacy. This chapter provides key aspects of information search and evaluation and discusses ways of developing information search and evaluation skills in and out of the language classroom.

2.1 Searching for information

The way we search for information has been dramatically changed since the introduction of the internet to the public in the early 1990s. Rather than visiting a library and using card catalogues in the library, we access the internet with digital devices and search for information by using web search engines anywhere anytime. We will see more changes as artificial intelligence (AI) technologies offer more conversational and complex responses to queries than a list of search results (Kelly, 2023). While there are serious concerns about the accuracy of information AI tools provide, AI-powered results are likely to make a great impact on the future of our online searches.

Information search is the process of locating or retrieving information to meet a specific information need (Mutta et al., 2014; Rowley, 2015). It is a key practice of digital literacy and a fundamental activity in digital spaces. It entails finding, accessing, browsing, navigating, filtering, organising, storing, retrieving, and managing information (Ferrari, 2013; Vuorikari et al., 2022). The Australian Curriculum, Assessment and Reporting Authority (ACARA) (2021) considered investigating as an element of the digital literacy learning continuum and presented four sub-elements:

- Locate information – Students curate information from digital resources. They effectively use research strategies to locate information and other resources. Students articulate their information and content needs, and effectively navigate information and content they encounter.
- Collect and collate data – Students understand how data can be generated, how to process data based on statistical understanding, and how to create or use artificial intelligence (AI) algorithms to recognise significant patterns and improve decision-making processes. They explore relevant data sets and read, manage and process data from a variety of sources.
- Interpret data – Students create and build knowledge by analysing data and communicating its meaning to others using various data visualisation tools. They present patterns, trends and analytical insights from data to facilitate problem-solving and decision making.
- Evaluate information – Students are careful and critical of the information that they encounter when online, and exhibit discernment in their evaluation of the reliability and credibility of online information. (p. 8)

Andretta (2005) emphasised that "e-learning needs to be underpinned by information literacy skills to foster independent learning, predispose the students towards a lifelong-learning attitude, and equip them with the ability to make informed decisions to deal effectively with information overload" (p. 182). In DigComp 2.2 (Vuorikari et al., 2022), information and data literacy is presented as its first competence area, which includes browsing, searching, and filtering data, information, and digital content; evaluating data, information, and digital content; and managing data, information, and digital content. Related to information search, DigComp 2.2 provides the following examples of knowledge, skills, and attitudes needed for digitally competent citizens, which are useful for language learners and teachers:

Knowledge
1. Knows that some online content in search result may not be open access or freely available and may require a fee or signing up for a service in order to access it.

2. Aware that online content that is available to users at no monetary cost is often paid for by advertising or by selling the user's data.
3. Aware that search results, social media activity streams and content recommendations on the internet are influenced by a range of factors. These factors include the search terms used, the context (e.g., geographical location), the device (e.g., laptop or mobile phone), local regulations (which sometimes dictate what can or cannot be shown), the behaviour of other users (e.g., trending searches or recommendations) and the user's past online behaviour across the internet.
4. Aware that search engines, social media, and content platforms often use AI algorithms to generate responses that are adapted to the individual user (e.g., users continue to see similar results or content). This is often referred to as "personalisation".
5. Aware that AI algorithms work in ways that are usually not visible or easily understood by users. This is often referred to as "black box" decision-making as it may be impossible to trace back how and why an algorithm makes specific suggestions or predictions.

Skills

6. Can choose the search engine that most likely meets one's information needs as different search engines can provide different results even for the same query.
7. Knows how to improve search results by using a search engine's advanced features (e.g., specifying exact phrase, language, region, date last updated).
8. Knows how to formulate search queries to achieve the desired output when interacting with conversational agents or smart speakers (e.g., *Siri, Alexa, Cortana, Google Assistant*), for example, recognising that, for the system to be able to respond as required, the query must be unambiguous and spoken clearly so that the system can respond.
9. Can make use of information presented as hyperlinks, in non-textual form (e.g., flowcharts, knowledge maps) and in dynamic representations (e.g., data).
10. Develops effective search methods for personal purposes (e.g., to browse a list of most popular films) and professional purposes (e.g., to find appropriate job advertisements).
11. Knows how to handle information overload and "infodemic" (i.e., increase of false or misleading information during a disease outbreak) by adapting personal search methods and strategies.

Attitudes

12. Intentionally avoids distractions and aims to avoid information overload when accessing and navigating information, data, and content.
13. Values tools designed to protect search privacy and other rights of users (e.g., browsers such as *DuckDuckGo*).
14. Weighs the benefits and disadvantages of using AI-driven search engines (e.g., while they might help users find the desired information, they may compromise privacy and personal data, or subject the user to commercial interests).
15. Concerned that much online information and content may not be accessible to people with a disability, for example, to users who rely on screen reader technologies to read aloud the content of a web page. (p. 10)

The use of online search engines is the most widely used information search strategy (Mutta et al., 2014; Singer et al., 2013). Among the search engines, *Google* is the most popular search engine and continues to expand its search services with generative AI capabilities (Sanderson et al., 2023). Through a survey of the use of online tools and professional development activities for learning about CALL, Son (2014b) confirmed that web search engines were the most frequently used online tool chosen by a group of CALL practitioners. In two studies on developing information-seeking competence in academic contexts, Mutta et al. (2014) investigated how their participants (native speakers of French and non-native speakers of French and Spanish) searched for relevant information online while using sources, keywords, strategies, and changes in language use (L1 and L2). They found that the participants developed several individual seeking paths and strategies to complete different tasks. The strategies the participants used included the use of different search possibilities available in *Google* and multilingual information retrieval strategies. The participants used different languages to find appropriate answers or translation equivalents and showed different seeking behaviours in the different tasks in line with their language backgrounds.

Teachers need to understand how to plan and construct a search strategy using appropriate keywords and/or advanced search functions available on search engines and online databases (e.g., Boolean operators such as AND, OR, and NOT) and how to apply criteria for evaluating the quality of information. They also need to understand copyright regulations and how to use online referencing tools and integrate online resources into an online learning environment (Mackenzie & Makin, 2003). They are encouraged to engage with informal learning activities such as self-exploration and connection with social networks to keep updating their knowledge and skills for using digital tools (Son, 2014b).

How can teaches support students to effectively find and select information online? Payton and Hague (2010) suggested the following ideas:

- Give students information about how to construct their web search so that they are more likely to find relevant information. Encourage them to be as specific as they can and to include several key words rather than just one when creating search terms.
- Students can also be taught to use Boolean terms such as AND, OR or AND NOT. For example, using AND in a search term (e.g., "critical thinking" AND "digital literacy") will ensure that search results include both phrases included in the search term. Putting their search term in quotation marks will ensure that results contain the complete and exact phrase they are looking for. Using the word 'define' followed by a colon and a search term (e.g., DEFINE: critical thinking) will return definitions of a particular word.
- Help students negotiate the large amount of information available on the internet by encouraging them to think about the purpose of their research and to select the information they need by engaging with the content of the material they are finding. They should be considering what information is relevant, suitable and helpful for their task.
- Students should also consider whether the information they find is reliable. Many teachers suggest that students check the information they are citing on at least three independent sites.
- Discuss the concept of plagiarism with your students and encourage them to cite their sources.
- Finally, students will need to think carefully about how they are going to use the information they find on the internet. How can it be repurposed and re-contextualised so that it fits their particular purpose?
- Once your students have begun developing their research skills, consider working with them to produce an 'effective internet research guide'. (p. 51)

Together with these ideas, teachers can design information search activities that can enhance both information literacy skills and language skills of their students while considering the students' proficiency levels and interests. The activities can be directly related to language learning objectives and reasonably challenging for the students. They can be designed to integrate language skills (e.g., reading articles, listening to interviews, writing summaries, delivering oral presentations) with authentic and culturally relevant materials and facilitate language learning with digital devices and tools (e.g., online databases, language learning websites, mobile apps, multimedia resources). They can be also used to train students to search for appropriate language learning activities for themselves.

Task 2.1

Search for information needed to answer the following questions:
Are you aware of different search engines?
Do you understand how search engines work and classify information?
Can social media platforms be used for online searches?

2.2 Evaluating information

We live with a plethora of information, which is available online at our fingertips. We also live with plenty of questions about the accuracy and reliability of the information we receive or find. It has become a requirement for us to select appropriate sources and evaluate the information carefully and critically before we accept and use it. Where does the information come from? Can the information be verified in other sources? We need knowledge and skills for effective information evaluation.

The ability to critically evaluate information is an essential online research skill. It is important for language learners and teachers to be able to critically assess the quality and credibility of information, make informed decisions about the information they use, and determine whether the information they use is trustworthy and relevant to their needs. Language learners need to be critical and reflective about how to find and locate information sources, analyse materials and resources (e.g., language learning apps, language learning websites, online dictionaries), and evaluate accuracy, credibility, and reliability of the sources. Their ability to evaluate information effectively can support and facilitate their language learning.

Darvin (2017) asserted that learners should develop a critical digital literacy to have the capacity to examine linguistic and non-linguistic features of digital media and verify information available in digital spaces. There are many online sources and websites that contain incorrect or misleading information (Peters & Frankoff, 2014). Successful online searches require the ability to use effective keyword search strategies (Kuiper & Volman,

2008), scan efficiently for relevant information (Rouet et al., 2011), and critically evaluate information found (Leu et al., 2015). Coiro (2017) suggested four dimensions of critical evaluation:

- Relevance: the information's level of importance to a particular reading purpose or explicitly stated need for that information
- Accuracy: the extent to which information contains factual and updated details that can be verified by consulting alternative and/or primary sources
- Bias/Perspective: the position or slant toward which an author shapes information
- Reliability: the information's level of trustworthiness based on information about the author and the publishing body (para. 3)

She also provided the following list of questions guiding students to think critically:

- Is this site relevant to my needs and purpose?
- What is the purpose of this site?
- Who created the information at this site, and what is this person's level of expertise?
- When was the information at this site updated?
- Where can I go to check the accuracy of this information?
- Why did this person or group put this information on the internet?
- Does the website present only one side of the issue, or are multiple perspectives provided?
- How are information and/or images at this site shaped by the author's stance?
- Is there anyone who might be offended or hurt by the information at this site?
- How can I connect these ideas to my own questions and interpretations? (para. 10)

Answers to these questions should be helpful for students to be able to determine whether the information they find is credible, reliable, and relevant to their needs.

Eshet-Alkalai (2004) highlighted that "the ability to evaluate and assess information properly has become a 'survival skill' for scholars and information consumers" (pp. 100–101). He added, "The main problems in evaluating information lie in the difficulty of assessing the credibility and originality of information and the professional integrity of its presentation" (p. 101). In Ferrari's (2013) self-assessment grid, the advanced level of information competence is illustrated as follows:

> I can use a wide range of strategies when searching for information and browsing on the internet. I am critical about the information I find and I can cross-check and assess its validity and credibility. I can filter and monitor the information I receive. I can apply different methods and tools to organise files, content and information. I can deploy a set of strategies for retrieving and managing the content I or others have organised and stored. I know whom to follow in online information sharing places (e.g., micro blogging). (p. 14)

Yaari et al. (2011) investigated what attributes Israeli university students used in order to assess Hebrew Wikipedia articles. They found that the most frequently mentioned evaluation criterion used by the students was the amount of information in an article (i.e., length), followed by the presence and quantity of external links. They affirmed that quality is a subjective concept that depends on the user's unique viewpoint. In a study of the formation of trust in digital information, specifically on a single Wikipedia article, Rowley and Johnson (2013) reported that, in trust formation, their participants used a range of factors (e.g., the expertise of the author, the appropriateness of the references, consistency with other information, recommendation by an expert) and verification procedures (e.g., comparison with other sources). In another study of K-12 school teachers' perceptions of the quality of information in Wikipedia, Meishar-Tal (2015) found that many teachers considered Wikipedia as an unreliable source and suggested that teachers should take an active approach to teach students to call on strategies for critical thinking and the evaluation and use of online information. In a different context, Peters and Frankoff (2014) conducted a survey of Chinese university students' information search strategies and digital scrapbooking strategies. They found that, although the students frequently used the web to find information for their assignments, the students were not efficient enough in their use of digital scrapbooking strategies. They suggested that teachers must be competent to teach digital scrapbooking strategies to their students. These studies highlight the importance of evaluating the reliability of information sources and training information search and evaluation strategies.

Task 2.2a

Find information online on a specific topic for your learning/teaching. Evaluate the information by using the following criteria: accuracy; authority; currency; objectivity; relevant; and reliability.

Task 2.2b

Share your most significant challenge you have in your digital context and discuss if there is anything that you feel affects your decision on the information you use.

2.3 Developing information search and evaluation skills

It is vital for teachers and students to develop information search and evaluation skills in digital language learning and teaching. Teachers need competence in searching for, evaluating, curating, organising, and sharing information and resources. They need to provide students with opportunities to use information search and evaluation skills and teach students effective information search and evaluation strategies. In practice, teachers can provide students with activities (e.g., information scavenger hunts, group research projects) to: find relevant information using search engines (e.g., *Google*, *Bing*); evaluate the quality, credibility, and relevance of information found (e.g., assessing the author, publication date, and reputation of the source); organise and curate information using digital tools such as *Dropbox*, *Google Drive*, *Microsoft OneDrive*, *Evernote*, *Google Docs*, *Microsoft OneNote*, *MindMeister*, *Padlet*, *Pinterest*, *Pocket*; and distinguish and manage different kinds of information (e.g., academic, professional, personal). They also need to offer guidance and feedback on students' information search and evaluation skills. Students can use the skills to access a wide range of relevant and reliable language resources for authentic language use. They can become independent learners who have a clear understanding of their information needs, search for online texts, audios, and videos in their target language, and use the resources to improve their language skills.

A variety of activities can be used for developing students' information search and evaluation skills in the context of language learning and teaching. For young language learners, for instance, gamified instructional design (e.g., Philpott & Son, 2022) can be considered with elements of gamification (e.g., points, timers, badges, leaderboards).

Example activities for developing information search and evaluation skills are given below.

Activity 2.1

Online scavenger hunt

Introduction	This activity aims to encourage and improve language learners' information search skills and problem-solving skills by using the idea of a scavenger hunt in online environments. It can be implemented as an individual activity or a group activity.
Target Language	Any language
Target Language Skills & Areas	Reading, writing, vocabulary, and grammar
Learner Levels	All levels
Activity Length	30–50 minutes
Preparation Time	30–50 minutes
Technical Requirements & Resources	A computer for each student or each group
	Zoom (https://zoom.us/) if implemented fully online
	Web search engines such as *Google* (https://www.google.com/) and *Bing* (https://www.bing.com/)
	Online word processors or note taking apps such as *Google Docs* (https://docs.google.com/), *Microsoft OneNote* (https://www.onenote.com/), and *Evernote* (https://evernote.com/)
	Padlet (https://padlet.com/)
Procedure	1. Make a list of items and challenges (e.g., topics, questions, clues) that students need to find and complete online.
	2. Guide students to use web search engines to search for specific information to find the items and complete the challenges.
	3. Guide the students to write their findings and selections on an online word processor or a note taking app.
	4. Ask the students to check off the items and challenges given in the list and submit their report to a *Padlet* board.
	5. Once completed, invite the students to discuss the results of the hunt and give feedback on them.

Continued....

Activity 2.1 *Continued....*

Options and Suggestions	• In a game mode, the teacher can use a countdown timer to help students keep track of time. After the timer runs out, the teacher can stop accepting submissions, look through each submission, and calculate points. • Audios and videos related to the topics, questions, and/or clues can be taken and used as part of the scavenger hunt where needed.

Activity 2.2

WebQuest

Introduction	This activity is an inquiry-based activity in which students are given a task to complete in a group with pre-selected online resources. It can promote students' critical thinking and collaboration skills.
Target Language	Any language
Target Language Skills & Areas	Reading, writing, listening, and speaking
Learner Levels	All levels
Activity Length	30–50 minutes
Preparation Time	30–50 minutes
Technical Requirements & Resources	A computer for each student or each group A set of topic-based resources selected and provided by the teacher *Google Docs* (https://docs.google.com/), *Google Maps* (https://maps.google.com/), *YouTube* (https://www.youtube.com/) *Padlet* (https://padlet.com/)
Procedure	1. Create a WebQuest with the following general structure: introduction, task, process, resources, evaluation, and conclusion. In doing so, define a topic area and choose a format for a WebQuest (e.g., a Word document, a Google Doc, a web page) and the right kind of websites and resources. Also, make the evaluation clear. 2. Implement the WebQuest. Ensure that students are aware of what they are doing and why they are doing it.

Continued....

Activity 2.2 *Continued....*

	3. Check the outcome of the WebQuest with the students. 4. Have a group discussion about what the students learnt about the topic, how their contribution to the group work was effective, and how they would like to improve their research and analytical skills.
Options and Suggestions	• Teachers need to review all sources in advance to make sure that the sources are appropriate and credible. • Teachers can use various online tools and resources for designing a WebQuest. They need to explore widely and provide a set of tools and resources helpful for students to complete the inquiry.

Activity 2.3

Online research project

Introduction	This activity gives students opportunities to find information on a particular topic online and create a presentation to share with others. Students are guided to include a discussion of sources they use and an evaluation of the credibility of the sources. The activity can be done individually or in a group.
Target Language	Any language
Target Language Skills & Areas	Reading, writing, listening, and speaking
Learner Levels	Intermediate to advanced level
Activity Length	30–50 minutes
Preparation Time	30–50 minutes
Technical Requirements & Resources	A computer for each student or each group
	Microsoft 365 (https://www.office.com/) or *Google Workspace* (https://workspace.google.com/)
	Web browsers such as *Microsoft Edge* (https://www.microsoft.com/edge), *Google Chrome* (https://chrome.google.com/), *Firefox* (https://www.mozilla.org/firefox), and *Safari* (https://www.apple.com/safari)
	Presentation tools such as *Canva* (https://www.canva.com/) and *Prezi* (https://prezi.com/)

Continued....

Activity 2.3 *Continued....*

Procedure	1. Choose a topic that interests students (e.g., being a digital citizen, researching a culture, planning an itinerary, creating a short podcast, creating a comic strip, writing a biography, reviewing a book, debating a significant issue). 2. Assign a research project to the students and explain the focal points of their research and presentation to them. 3. Set research time and presentation time. Ensure that the students understand what they need to do and why they do it. 4. Check the students' progress and give guidance and feedback whenever needed. 5. Ask the students to submit and present their outcomes. 6. Have a group discussion about what the students learnt from their research and how they would like to improve their research and evaluation skills.
Options and Suggestions	• The research project should be appropriate for students' proficiency levels. • The teacher can guide students to include and use multimedia resources in their presentation.

Activity 2.4

Fake news

Introduction	This activity allows students to raise their awareness of fake news, improve the ability to evaluate information, and develop critical thinking skills. It includes news articles with various levels of credibility and discussion questions for the evaluation of the information. It can be done individually or in a group.
Target Language	Any language
Target Language Skills & Areas	Reading, writing, listening, and speaking
Learner Levels	Intermediate to advanced level
Activity Length	30–50 minutes
Preparation Time	30–50 minutes

Continued....

Activity 2.4 *Continued....*

Technical Requirements & Resources	A computer for each student or each group
	Microsoft 365 (https://www.office.com/) or *Google Workspace* (https://workspace.google.com/)
	Web browsers such as *Microsoft Edge* (https://www.microsoft.com/edge), *Google Chrome* (https://chrome.google.com/), *Firefox* (https://www.mozilla.org/firefox), and *Safari* (https://www.apple.com/safari)
Procedure	1. Create a game where students are given a series of news articles, images, and web pages in the target language and asked to determine which ones are real and which ones are fake.
	2. Have a brief discussion about fake news with the students.
	3. Present some resources that help the students understand the psychology and dangers of fake news. For example: ClickView - The digital literacy series: Fake news (https://www.clickview.com.au/free-teaching-resources/fake-news/); BBC - Help your students spot false news (https://www.bbc.co.uk/programmes/articles/4fRwvHcfr5hYMMltFqvP6qF/help-your-students-spot-false-news).
	4. Present the news articles, images, and web pages and ask the students to study them, using a set of questions to review.
	5. Check the students' choices or votes and give feedback on them while going through each news article, each image, and each web page.
	6. Ask the students to find other fake news currently being spread online and make a list of their findings.
	7. Have a group discussion about what the students learnt from the activity and how they would like to improve their ability to identify fake news.
Options and Suggestions	• The news articles used in the activity should be appropriate for students' proficiency levels.
	• Students can present their findings in a written report or a group oral presentation.

Task 2.3

Make a list of skills that you think important for information search and evaluation and then design online activities that could be useful for developing the skills.

Discussion Questions

1. How do you find information online (e.g., websites, blogs, wikis, social media services)?
2. What search engine or tool do you find the most useful and why?
3. What search strategies do you use to find and access appropriate and relevant information?
4. How do you evaluate the information you find online?
5. How do you make critical judgement when evaluating information and sources?
6. How do you assess currency, reliability, and authority of information?
7. How do you identify and rectify logical fallacies and errors?
8. How much do you think biases affect your judgement about information encountered on the web?
9. How do you reflect on your own literacy practices in information search and evaluation?
10. How can we effectively manage information in digital environments?

3
Creation

The creation of digital content is an increasingly important part of digital literacy and involves creating meaning through text, images, sounds, and/or videos in digital environments. It allows individuals to present their work and express their ideas and views in digital formats (e.g., a blog, a graphic, a website, a podcast, a video, a digital presentation). Language learners are expected to develop their digital competence and have the ability to create digital content while demonstrating their language skills in their target language. Language teachers need to design and use practical activities, materials, and resources that help language learners meet the expectation. This chapter explores digital content creation and discusses how to develop digital content creation skills.

3.1 Creating content

We produce and share digital content with digital devices we use. The content is created to reach target audiences and drives our communication with others. We come out with ideas, create written, audio, or visual content based on the ideas, and make it accessible to others in various formats such as social networking service (SNS) messages, forum posts, blog posts, web pages, e-books, images, podcasts, and videos. As more and more digital creation tools are introduced and available to us, it has become easier to create digital content and share it with others for specific purposes.

Digital content creation is the process of creating content in digital contexts. It requires creative ideas, critical thinking, subject knowledge, and technical skills. Ferrari's (2013) digital competence areas include information, communication, content creation, safety, and problem solving. Among them, content creation has four specific competences to consider: developing content; integrating and re-elaborating; copyright and licences; and programming. It involves creating and editing new content (from word processing to images and video); integrating and re-elaborating previous knowledge and content; dealing with and applying intellectual property rights and licences; and producing creative expressions, media outputs, and programming. In her self-assessment grid, the advanced level of content creation is explained as follows:

> I can produce digital content in different formats, platforms and environments. I can use a variety of digital tools for creating original multimedia outputs. I can mash-up existing items of content to create new ones. I know how different types of licences apply to the information and resources I use and create. I can interfere with (open) programmes, modify, change or write source code. I can code and programme in several languages. I understand the systems and functions that are behind programmes. (p. 14)

Similarly, Lonan (2021) pointed out that digital content creation requires specific competences in "digital content development, editing and integration, copyright and licences, elementary programming skills, and creative usage of digital technologies" (para. 21). The Australian Curriculum, Assessment and Reporting Authority (ACARA) (2021), on the other hand, highlighted three sub-elements of creating:

- Plan and design – Students use digital tools to plan and manage a process that considers design constraints and risks.
- Create content – Students execute plans for the design of digital content and products based on needs, practicality, efficiency and functionality. They develop, test and refine models to create original products or ethically repurpose or remix resources into new content.
- Respect intellectual property – Students understand the ethical and legal responsibilities around ownership and remixing of online content, for example, plagiarism, copyright, fair use and licensing. They demonstrate responsibility and respect for others by protecting their own digital creations and crediting others' content when appropriate. (pp. 8–9)

Ivers and Barron (2015) argued that a benefit of digital content creation is that "it allows students to construct and communicate knowledge in various ways" (p. 7). They added, "Digital content creation also encourages group work and social interaction, but it does not require a uniform experience for all students" (p. 7). Based on Gardner's (1983, 1999) theory of multiple intelligences, they presented a table correlating each intelligence with student behaviours and roles in digital content creation (see Table 3.1).

Table 3.1 *Roles of Multiple Intelligence in Digital Content Creation (adapted from Ivers & Barron, 2015, p. 8)*

Intelligence	Observed Student Behaviours	Recommended Roles in Digital Content Creation
Linguistic	Loves to read books, write, and tell stories; good memory for names, dates, and trivia; communicates well	Gather and develop text for project; provide narration; keep journal of group progress
Logical-Mathematical	Excels in math; has strong problem-solving skills; enjoys playing strategy games and working on logic puzzles	Design flowchart; write scripting and programming code; develop navigation routes
Spatial	Needs a mental or physical picture to best understand things; draws figures that are advanced for age; doodles a lot	Create graphics, animation, and other visual media for project; design layout
Body-Kinesthetic	Excels in one or more sports; good fine-motor skills; tendency to move around, touch things, gesture	Keyboard information; manipulate objects with mouse; operate multimedia equipment
Musical	Remembers melodies; recognizes when music is off-key; has a good singing voice; plays an instrument; hums a lot	Identify works for content integration; create musical score for project; input audio/sound effects
Interpersonal	Enjoys socializing with peers; has leadership skills; has good sense of empathy and concern for others	Coordinate group efforts; help set group goals; help solve group disputes
Intrapersonal	Has strong sense of self; is confident; prefers working alone; has high self-esteem; displays independence	Conduct independent research to share with teammates; pilot test multimedia projects; lead multimedia presentations
Naturalist	Enjoys the outdoors, plants, and animals; easily recognizes and classifies things within his or her environment	Collect outside elements for incorporation into projects; organise project work

In an English as a foreign language (EFL) context, Hung (2019) explored cognitive and metacognitive skills EFL learners at a Taiwanese university developed when creating digital stories, which combined narratives with images, sounds, animations and videos. He found that the learners frequently employed cognitive skills (e.g., analysing, generating, information gathering, organising) and metacognitive skills (e.g., planning, monitoring, goal setting, evaluating, appraisal) when composing multimodal texts. He also found that highly engaged learners employed significantly more cognitive and metacognitive skills than less engaged learners. He concluded that the cognitive and metacognitive skills developed by the learners can serve to practise multiliteracies. Based on a create-to-learn paradigm in a different context, Liu et al. (2018) examined the effects of a digital storytelling approach on elementary school students' language learning motivation and creativity performance. They found that the digital storytelling approach had a positive impact on the students' motivation and performance and reported that the students' motivation in language learning were closely related to the creativity level of their digital stories.

Payton and Hague (2010) suggested a range of activities that support teachers in integrating the development of students' digital literacy into curriculum teaching with free digital tools. They contended that becoming digitally literate involves being active in using digital tools and in creating and producing meaning and knowledge in different digital formats (e.g., animations, podcasts, videos). Hague and Payton (2010) concurred that digital technologies provide an array of opportunities for learners to be creative and create their own digital content and meaning in cultural and social contexts. They presented the following list of tips for developing creativity in the classroom (informed by Fautley & Savage, 2007), which can be useful for teachers in creating activities for their students:

- providing regular opportunities for using creativity in the classroom and for creating outputs in a wide variety of formats and modes
- either setting or asking students to define a clear purpose and audience for any creative output
- supporting students to carefully plan their creative work and access the resources they will need for it
- exploring with students the needs of particular audiences and how to tailor content accordingly
- establishing success criteria with students and setting achievable goals
- supporting students to explore ideas and to engage in independent and creative thinking, allowing them to take control of their own learning and their own creative process

- identifying creative abilities in students, giving them opportunities to use their individual abilities and rewarding them
- reviewing work in progress and providing feedback
- looking at examples of other creative outputs, media or digital texts in a particular subject and asking students to assess how successful they are and analyse how they convey information and meaning
- providing students with a structure in which to use their creativity (e.g., making sure they have a clearly-defined purpose, audience, time-scale, assessment criteria and plan) (p. 26)

A massive amount of user-generated content is available online (e.g., social media, blogs, wikis, discussion forums). For example, *YouTube* offers a complex, multi-authored, and multicultural virtual space (Benson, 2017; Chen, 2020) and presents user-generated videos and comments through a participatory culture (Jenkins et al., 2016). Yeh and Swinehart (2022) asserted that the expansion of user-generated content from online participatory cultures such as social networks raises the need for social media literacy training for language learners who need to develop their language abilities effectively and efficiently in online social environments. Based on the analysis of data from a pre-task questionnaire and a post-task questionnaire with a group of international students in an English language course at an American university, they suggested the development of a social media literacy training model that offers language learners cognitive competencies, technical competencies, and sociocultural pragmatics. In training the learners, the training model would need to respond to different backgrounds and needs of the learners.

Task 3.1

Create digital content in the format you are familiar with and discuss the value of the content in your language learning and teaching context.

3.2 Developing digital content creation skills

Digital content creation supports language learners to be creative, analytical, communicative, collaborative, innovative, and competent in using digital tools. It also poses challenges for language learners, particularly who may not have sufficient language proficiency or digital competence to create digital artefacts confidently. To overcome the challenges, there is a need for language teachers to provide language learners with opportunities to learn how to use digital tools and software effectively and engage in meaningful and pertinent content creation activities. Language learners also need guidance and support in dealing with language-related issues such as grammar, vocabulary, and the style of writing in the target language and raising cultural awareness and intercultural understanding. Language teachers can consider incorporating content creation skills into the language teaching curriculum by developing and using content creation activities in language lessons.

Example activities for developing content creation skills in the language classroom are shown below.

Activity 3.1

Blogging challenge

Introduction	This activity is designed to help students learn about the basics and logistics of blogging. It encourages students to actively participate in blog writing as reflective learners and creators.
Target Language	Any language
Target Language Skills & Areas	Reading, writing, vocabulary, and grammar
Learner Levels	All levels
Activity Length	50–60 minutes
Preparation Time	50–60 minutes
Technical Requirements & Resources	A computer for each student
	A blogging platform such as *Blogger* (https://www.blogger.com/) or *WordPress* (https://wordpress.com/)
	Web search engines such as *Google* (https://www.google.com/) and *Bing* (https://www.bing.com/)
Procedure	1. Choose a blogging platform.
	2. Select a blog name and template.
	3. Provide a list of challenges (e.g., topics, questions) that students need to choose and write about in a blog.
	4. Guide students to use web search engines to search for specific information when needed.
	5. Guide the students to write engaging content and post it.
	6. Encourage the students to make comments on other students' posts.
	7. Invite the students to discuss the blog posts and give feedback on them.

Continued....

Activity 3.1 *Continued....*

Options and Suggestions	• The teacher can consider further steps and guide students to promote their blog posts online.
	• Relevant images and other types of media content can be suggested and used in blog posts.

Activity 3.2

Video creation

Introduction	This activity allows students to learn about online video creation and pay their attention to particular linguistic elements, forms, or features of their target language through creating a video.
Target Language	Any language
Target Language Skills & Areas	Speaking, listening, and writing
Learner Levels	All levels
Activity Length	80–90 minutes
Preparation Time	80–90 minutes
Technical Requirements & Resources	A computer for each student or each group
	Cloud-based video creation platforms such as *Animoto* (https://animoto.com/) and *Renderforest* (https://www.renderforest.com/)
	Google Docs (https://docs.google.com/), *YouTube* (https://www.youtube.com/)
Procedure	1. Introduce a video creation platform to students.
	2. Ask the students to go to the website and watch some example videos provided by the website.
	3. Give the students instructions on what they need to do.
	4. Guide the students to create a short video on a specific topic in a specific format (or a topic and a format of their choice).
	5. Provide guidance and feedback on their work to produce a video that is engaging and appealing.
	6. Encourage them to share their video with other students through a class website, a class wiki, or a class blog if appropriate.
	7. Have a group discussion about their experience with the video creation activity.

Continued....

Activity 3.2 *Continued....*

Options and Suggestions	• Teachers are encouraged to explore more video creation and presentation tools online for different types of language learning activities. • Teachers can make explicit links between language lessons and videos created by students themselves.

Activity 3.3

Digital portfolio

Introduction	This activity gives students opportunities to create their e-portfolios and showcase their work and skills online. It involves organising and planning material and selecting and arranging content to present to a particular audience.
Target Language	Any language
Target Language Skills & Areas	Reading, writing, vocabulary, and grammar
Learner Levels	Intermediate to advanced level
Activity Length	50–60 minutes
Preparation Time	50–60 minutes
Technical Requirements & Resources	A computer for each student or each group Digital portfolio tools/systems such as *Google Sites* (https://sites.google.com/), *Mahara* (https://mahara.org/), *Microsoft OneNote* (https://www.onenote.com/), and *Padlet* (https://padlet.com/)
Procedure	1. Introduce a digital portfolio tool to students. 2. Assign the students a task to create their digital portfolio. The task can include a collection of their work, personal statements, and learning achievements. 3. Guide the students to understand what they need to do and how they can do it. 4. Check the students' progress and give guidance and feedback whenever needed. 5. Ask the students to submit and present their portfolio. 6. Have a group discussion about what the students learnt from the activity.

Continued....

Activity 3.3 *Continued....*

Options and Suggestions	• The teacher is encouraged to explore a range of functionality of digital portfolio platforms before the activity. • The teacher can make clear links between different stages of learning through students' portfolios.

Activity 3.4

Website design

Introduction	This activity helps students become familiar with website creation tools and provides them with opportunities to create a website for a specific purpose.
Target Language	Any language
Target Language Skills & Areas	Reading, writing, listening, and speaking
Learner Levels	Intermediate to advanced level
Activity Length	50–60 minutes
Preparation Time	50–60 minutes
Technical Requirements & Resources	A computer for each student or each group Website builders such as *Google Sites* (https://sites.google.com/), *Weebly* (https://www.weebly.com/), *Webnode* (https://www.webnode.com/), and *Wix* (https://www.wix.com/)
Procedure	1. Introduce a website builder to students. 2. Assign the students a task to create their own website. The task can include designing a self-introduction page, building a language learning page, or presenting information relevant to their target language. 3. Guide the students to understand what they need to do and how they can do it. 4. Check the students' progress and give guidance and feedback whenever needed. 5. Ask the students to submit and present their website address. 6. Have a group discussion about their websites created through the activity.

Continued....

Activity 3.4 *Continued....*

Options and Suggestions	• The teacher can consider using other types of website creation tools in different formats.
• Students can present and describe their websites in a written report or a group oral presentation.

In addition to the creation activities above, the following activities can be also considered:

- Creating an animation with *Animaker* (https://www.animaker.com/) or *Do Ink* (https://www.doink.com/)
- Creating an e-book with *Book Creator* (https://bookcreator.com/)
- Creating an online database with *Airtable* (https://www.airtable.com/)
- Creating a podcast with *Podomatic* (https://www.podomatic.com/)
- Creating a wiki with *PBworks* (https://www.pbworks.com/wikis.html)
- Creating a word cloud with *WordArt.com* (https://wordart.com/) or *WordClouds.com* (https://www.wordclouds.com/)

Additional Activities

The following example activity (Santosa & Ivone, 2020) demonstrates how a digital creation activity can be part of an integrated lesson.

Activity Title	Virtual reality-infused language learning
Introduction	Virtual Reality (VR) technology has reached a point in which it can be used for realistic learning. It allows learners to visit places they cannot physically visit and do things they cannot do within the constrain of schools and homes.
Target Language	English
Target Language Skills & Areas	Integrated skills, vocabulary and grammar
Learner Levels	Beginner-intermediate level
Activity Aims	This activity aims to provide learners with opportunities to collaboratively use the target language and technology to research and discuss a topic and create a topic-related poster.

Continued....

Additional Activities *Continued....*

Activity Length	180 minutes
Preparation Time	60 minutes (time for the teacher to prepare for materials)
Technical Requirements & Resources	1. Downloaded VR application of Animals of Nusantara (AoN) from http://bit.ly/sldVRapps 2. VR glasses 3. Android smartphones 4. *Wakelet* (https://wke.lt/w/s/dLD37S) 5. *Padlet* (https://padlet.com/mhsantosa/animals)

Procedure	1. Do a pre-activity
	  a. Students brainstorm the topic of endangered animals.
	  b. Students watch a video about tigers (https://youtu.be/FK3dav4bA4s) and respond to guided questions.
	  c. Divide the class into four groups and each group is assigned a role as (1) government representatives, (2) NGO/activists, (3) citizens, or (4) zookeepers.
	  d. Each group members respond from the perspectives of their roles.
	2. Research the topic from different perspectives
	  a. In their groups, students learn about endangered animals from AoN VR (alternatively, pictures, animations and/or videos).
	  b. Students take notes on important information on the animals' habitat, numbers, food, etc.
	  c. Students do a crowd curation activity in *Wakelet* (https://wke.lt/w/s/dLD37S) to gather more information.
	3. Put things together
	  a. Based on the roles, students write important points on an online wall such as *Padlet* (https://padlet.com/mhsantosa/animals).
	  b. Students visit each other's wall and give feedback.
	  c. In their groups, students discuss the feedback given.
	  d. In their groups, students list 3 main points for a virtual oral class presentation.

Continued....

Additional Activities *Continued....*

                    4. Create a poster
                        a. Students observe the assessment rubric for a poster project.
                        b. Students create a poster with the theme of "Saving Endangered Animals" individually.
                        c. Students may use digital tools such as *Canva* (https://www.canva.com) or *Venngage* (https://venngage.com) for poster creation.
                        d. Students exchange their work and give feedback to their friends' posters.
                        e. After the revision, students set up a gallery wall.
                    5. Reflect on the learning activities with questions, such as "What have you learned about endangered animals?" and "If you have one animal to save, what will it be and why?"

Options and Suggestions

- VR glasses are optional, but learners may experience more engaging learning when they are used. (Avoid using them for more than 5 minutes as students may feel dizzy.)
- Students can use any applications or software they are familiar with when designing their poster.
- Mind mapping activity can be inserted in Procedure 2 after the crowd curation activity.
- Instead of creating their own individual posters, they can also work in pairs or small groups.
- Students may review each other's poster during the process.
- A digital art gallery can be set up for displaying students' posters.

Justification

This VR-infused language learning activity focuses on cooperative learning that cultivates various 21st century skills. Cooperative learning that refers to a tradition of principles and techniques, which support teachers in facilitating interaction among learners, works best when learning task design encourages to interact (Dixon et al., 2020; Johnson et al., 2007). The VR-infused activity facilitates learners in interacting not only with the learning content and instructional media but also with their peers as well as teachers. It is important that cooperative

Continued....

Additional Activities *Continued....*

learning includes individual accountability (Johnson et al., 2007), which encourages each learner to do their fair share toward the success of their group. Another reason for individual activity – before and/or after cooperating with peers – is that the success of cooperative learning lies not in what the group does but in what each group member learns (Jacobs & Ivone, 2020).

The term 21st century skills refers to a broad set of knowledge, skills, work habits, and character traits that are believed to be critically important to success in future careers and workplaces (Mercado, 2017). The skills are varied but share some common themes that are based on providing effective learning in educational contexts. The pedagogies involve higher order thinking skills and learning dispositions represented in 4Cs, namely collaboration, communication, critical thinking, and creativity (Santosa, 2019).

References and Further Reading

Dixon, S., Shewell, J., & Crandell, J. (2020). *100 ways to teach language online*. Wayzgoose Press.

Jacobs, G. M., & Ivone, F. M. (2020). Infusing cooperative learning in distance education. *TESL-EJ, 24*(1), 1-15. http://www.tesl-ej.org/wordpress/issues/volume24/ej93/ej93a1/

Johnson, D. W., Johnson, R. T., & Holubec, E. J. (2007). *Nuts & bolts of cooperative learning* (2nd ed.). Interaction Book Company.

Mercado, L. A. (2017). *Technology for the language classroom: Creating a 21st century learning experience*. Palgrave Macmillan.

Santosa, M. H. (2019). Introduction to core skills and its best practices in the Indonesian classrooms. In M. H. Santosa (Ed.), *Penerapan core skills di kelas-kelas di Indonesia* (pp. 723). Azizah Publishing.

(Santosa & Ivone, 2020, pp. 75–78)

The following example activity (Bensal, 2023) shows how the creation of a digital poster can be connected with academic English writing.

Activity Title	Creating an academic poster
Introduction	Teachers seldom suggest an online tool or software to materialize an academic poster, which is a "hybrid of a published paper and an oral presentation" (Miller, 2007, p. 311). Incorporating the creation of an e-poster in the research writing process can address students' common writing weaknesses – verbosity and unparalleled ideas.
Target Language	English
Target Language Skills & Areas	Writing
Learner Levels	Senior high school students of ESL/EFL with basic knowledge of academic writing
Activity Aims	This activity aims to help students transform their research paper into an academic poster, practice brevity in expressing their ideas, and observe parallelism.
Activity Length	90 minutes (15 minutes for preparing; 30 minutes for writing highlights for each research section; 30 minutes for poster making; and 15 minutes for debriefing)
Preparation Time	15 minutes (allocated for signing up to Canva and conceptualizing ideas on creating an e-poster)
Technical Requirements & Resources	*Canva* (https://www.canva.com/); *YouTube*: How to use Canva (https://www.youtube.com/watch?v=zJSgUx5K6V0)
Procedure	1. Ask students to divide their writing into sections (e.g., introduction, research questions, methodology). 2. Provide only highlights per section: one phrase or one sentence per bullet point; phrases must be no more than 5 words; sentences must be no more than 15 words; and bullet points per section must be no more than 3. 3. Guide the students to: (1) open the *Canva* (https://www.canva.com/) website and login; (2) click "create a design" and choose "poster" for the dimensions; (3) select a template that best suits their research paper's theme; (4) type their research title and name on top; (5) customize their e-poster layout; (6) remove unnecessary words or phrases; (7) proofread their work (e.g., spelling, punctuation); (8) save and download their design (PDF, JPG, or PNG); and (9) submit their poster to the teacher.

Continued....

Options and Suggestions	• Students may combine or use other applications (e.g., *Photoshop*, *Paint Tool Sai 2*, *Kanban*). • Students may opt to choose a blank canvas and divide it into sections needed for the poster through inserting straight lines, curved lines, and rectangles. • The teacher may ask students to create a reference page on a separate *Google Docs* (https://docs.google.com/), generate a QR code redirecting to the *Google Docs*, and download the QR code and attach it to the poster. • Students will understand the *Canva* application and the importance of brevity and parallelism more once they do their poster, so be a little patient with them and let them really experience it.
Justification	Being novice writers, students have the tendency to write in verbose and confusing ways. They have the impression that the longer the work, the better it is (Alsalami, 2022). Even despite several revisions, students may still not get a full grasp of their work and the essence of brevity (Scott, 2014) and parallelism (Watling, 2015). However, when they are exposed to creating an e-poster from their research papers, they are transported in a different genre of academic writing process (Romadlon, 2019). By creating an e-poster, students are given the chance to properly divide their work into several sections accompanied with the most important information in the form of a few phrases and sentences only. As they create several sections, they can easily identify parts that need to be parallel with each other. This activity trains them to retain only the most essential ideas because of the prescribed number of words given by the teacher. Hence, it can improve their "editing, succinctness, and the ability to synthesize the literature" (Cyr, 2017, p. A46). Conciseness is essential in any scientific paper, especially for a research poster. With the help of a more sophisticated tool (like Canva) in creating an e-poster, research presenters can achieve clarity and persuasiveness through the power of parallel structure and brevity (Watling, 2015).

Continued....

Chapter 3 **49**

References and Further Reading

Alsalami, A. I. (2022). Challenges of short sentence writing encountered by first-year Saudi EFL undergraduate students. *Arab World English Journal, 13*(1), 534-549.

Bensal, E. R. (2021, August 14). Sustainable communication strategies. https://www.edwinarbensal.com/post/sustainable-communication-strategies

Cyr, N. E. (2017). "Brevity is the soul of wit": Use of a stepwise project to teach concise scientific writing. *Journal of Undergraduate Neuroscience Education, 16*(1), A46-A51. https://www.funjournal.org/wp-content/uploads/2017/09/june-16-46.pdf?x36670

Gehred, A. P. (2020). Canva. *Journal of the Medical Library Association, 108*(2), 338-340. https://doi.org/10.5195/jmla.2020.940

Miller, J. E. (2007, February). Preparing and presenting effective research posters. *Health Services Research, 42*(1p1), 311-328. https://doi.org/10.1111/j.1475-6773.2006.00588.x

Nordquist, R. (2017, April 18). Brevity in speech and writing. *ThoughtCo.* https://www.thoughtco.com/brevity-speech-and-writing-1689037

Romadlon, F. N. (2019). *Online poster presentation to activate students' writing ability.* https://eprints.umk.ac.id/10160/1/Turnitin%20LOOW%204%202014.pdf

Scott, R. (2014). The art of brevity. *Visual Arts Research, 40*(78), 121-123.

Watling, C. (2015). The power of parallel structure. *Perspectives on Medical Education, 4*(6), 329-330. https://doi.org/10.1007/s40037-015-0227-3

Ziovo. (2020, March 21). How to use Canva for beginners (Canva tutorial 2020) [Video file]. YouTube. https://www.youtube.com/watch?v=zJSgUx5K6V0

(Bensal, 2023, pp. 48–50)

Task 3.2

Explore a range of digital content creation tools and make a list of tools you would like to use in your context.

Discussion Questions

1. How do you define creativity in language learning and teaching?
2. What is content creation in digital environments?
3. How can engaging digital content be created in the language classroom?
4. What digital content creation tools are you familiar with?
5. What is it to be digitally creative in language learning and teaching?
6. How does digital content creation affect your language teaching?
7. What creative ideas do you have for facilitating students' digital content creation skills?
8. How might creating an e-book support students' language knowledge and skills?
9. How might creating a video support students' language knowledge and skills?
10. How do you measure the quality of digital content?

4
Communication

Digital communication occurs in our daily lives. It involves email, blogs, podcasts, text messaging, voice chats, and/or video conferencing. It uses a variety of online communication tools (e.g., *Gmail* [https://mail.google.com/], *Microsoft Outlook* [https://outlook.live.com/], *Skype* [https://www.skype.com/], *Zoom* [https://zoom.us/]) and social networking tools (e.g., *Facebook* [https://www.facebook.com/], *Instagram* [https://www.instagram.com/], *LinkedIn* [https://www.linkedin.com/], *Twitter* [https://twitter.com/]) to reach other individuals or a specific audience. It is a key element of digital literacy as all activities in digital environments involve digital communication, exchanging information and ideas. The ability to communicate effectively in digital networks is essential for language learners and teachers. Language learners need to use or adapt their target language properly to be a good communicator in synchronous and asynchronous online communication. This chapter explores digital communication and discusses how to develop digital communication skills.

4.1 Communicating online

Digital technologies offer opportunities for authentic communication with others in different time zones and locations. We regularly use communication tools such as email, short message services (SMSs), SNSs, and video conferencing services to communicate with others in digital environments. We develop, maintain, and update our personal and professional networks through digital communication. Interaction can occur synchronously (at the same time) or asynchronously (at different times) in digital communication. Effective interpersonal communication skills enable us to express our thoughts clearly and improve our relationships with others.

Digital communication is the process of interacting with digital technologies. It requires communication skills, which allow individuals to engage and communicate in a range of digital formats (e.g., online discussion forums, social media platforms). The efficient, effective, and appropriate use of CMC tools or digital communication tools is needed to communicate clearly and coherently. Belshaw (2014) stated that "communicating effectively using a particular digital technology involves knowing, understanding and applying certain norms and assumptions" (p. 50) and underlined that the communicative element of digital literacies is of crucial importance.

In a study of synchronous computer-mediated communication (SCMC), Coyle and Reverte Prieto (2017) investigated young EFL learners' interactional strategy use and lexical acquisition during text-based online chat and reported that the learners' participation in SCMC raised their awareness of gaps in their lexical knowledge. In another study of SCMC, Jung et al. (2019) investigated university students' perceptions of the effectiveness of SCMC interactions for their EFL learning and intercultural competence development in a cross-cultural project. The students from three countries (i.e., Korea, Japan, and Taiwan) were engaged with video chat sessions, completed an online questionnaire, and participated in interviews. Jung et al. found that the students' attention to language and their attention to culture were significant predictors of positive attitudes toward SCMC. With a different focus, Young and Son (2023) explored SCMC and task-based learning in an EFL classroom setting in Japan. They compared text chat and voice chat using three tasks (i.e., opinion exchange, dictogloss, and problem-solving) and found that task design features such as input, time allocation, and goal orientation could influence learner uptake in the EFL classroom.

Looking at the use of online discussion groups in a postgraduate course for language teachers, Son (2002) identified patterns of participant-participant interactions and reported that the participants contributed primarily in the forms of fully and partially task-focused messages while the messages mainly consisted of task-based answers and interactive contributions. He concluded that online discussions were useful for CALL teacher training as they provided language teachers with practical experiences of CMC and communication channels for sharing ideas, comments, questions, and resources with their fellow teachers. Subsequently, Son (2006) also found similar results and confirmed that CMC could provide teachers with communication channels for sharing ideas and resources and collaborating with others.

Lotherington and Ronda (2014) expressed the view that digital communication "extends semiotic possibilities beyond the traditional walls of language: different media and modalities are spliced to create new meanings" (p. 18). They proposed a digital framework of communicative competencies, which include multimedia competency, collaborative communication, agentive participation, and multitasking competency. In their reimagining communicative competence, particularly, collaborative communication involves "collaborative meaning production, including multiple authorship; ongoing learning through critical dialogue and engagement; recognizing and harnessing machine mediation; and social participation in global forums" (p. 19).

According to the Australian Curriculum, Assessment and Reporting Authority (ACARA) (2021), communicating means that "students recognise different types of peer-to-peer communication and collaboration strategies, tools and formats, and decide which methods are most effective for individual or collaborative goals" (p. 8). Ferrari's (2013) digital competences in communication include: interacting through technologies; sharing information and content; engaging in online citizenship; collaborating through digital channels; netiquette; and managing digital identity. In her self-assessment grid, the advanced level of communication is described as follows:

> I am engaged in the use of a wide range of tools for online communication (emails, chats, SMS, instant messaging, blogs, micro-blogs, SNS). I can apply the various aspects of online etiquette to different digital communication spaces and contexts. I have developed strategies to discover inappropriate behaviour. I can adopt digital modes and ways of communication that best fit the purpose. I can tailor the format and ways of communication to my audience. I can manage the different types of communication I receive. I can actively share information, content and resources with others through online communities, networks and collaboration platforms. I am actively participating in online spaces. I know how to get actively engaged in online participation and I can use several different online services. I frequently and confidently use several digital collaboration tools and means to collaborate with others in the production and sharing of resources, knowledge and content. I can manage several digital identities according to the context and purpose. I can monitor the information and data I produce through my online interaction. I know how to protect my digital reputation. (p. 14)

Hull and Stornaiuolo (2010) made a point that young people require high-powered versions of literacy to participate actively in their educational and social contexts. They stated that social networks have offered "many opportunities for youth to situate themselves and their local worlds in relation to others and experiment with self-making through the hybridization of multimedia artifacts" (p. 92) and argued that youth should develop sensitivities to the meaning-making practices of others when they communicate with others via social media. Particularly for children, Rodríguez-de-Dios and Igartua (2016) proposed the implementation of a digital literacy intervention to address and manage risks of interactive communication (e.g., cyberbullying, sexual harassment, contact with strangers). Their model of digital literacy consisted of five skills: technological or instrumental skill; communication skill; information skill; critical skill; and security skill. They asserted that, by increasing children's digital competences, children can address the risks of interactive communication effectively and safely.

Hague and Payton (2010) offered the following tips for developing effective communication skills:

- Encourage students to distinguish between effective and non-effective communication and to discuss what constitutes effective communication
- Give students adequate time to plan any form of communication and including time for students to regularly review their work
- Make sure students are aware of what audience they are communicating with and encourage them to think about the needs of that audience
- Try to create real audiences for students – this may mean developing relationships with the local community or with other teachers.
- Make sure that when students communicate to an audience, they are given feedback – this can help students to improve their communication and also means that the audience has an active role to play. If the audience is the rest of the class as a whole, it can also help to encourage students to listen to others and provide opportunities for peer teaching and peer assessment. (p. 33)

These tips are useful for teachers in creating and using digital communication activities that can enhance language learning. Through the activities using digital communication tools, students can have engaging learning experiences with real audience and authentic materials such as videos, podcasts, and social media. They can practice their language skills and learn from each other. They can also explore cultural differences, increase cultural awareness, and develop intercultural communicative competence (ICC). The concept of ICC has been broadly discussed in the literature in relation to a range of terms such as communicative competence, cross-cultural communication, international communication, intercultural communication, intercultural competence, and intercultural sensitivity (e.g., Bennett, 1993; Byram, 1997; Deardorff, 2006; Fantini & Tirmizi,

2006). While it entails more than a combination of awareness, understanding, attitudes, knowledge, and skills, ICC might be simply defined as the ability to communicate appropriately and effectively in intercultural situations. Given that its emphasis is given to competence in communication and interaction across cultures, ICC needs to be developed and improved through formal and informal learning and a variety of experiences. Liaw (2019) investigated a group of EFL learners' intercultural communication in an open social virtual environment and reported that the learners perceived the social and physical presences afforded by a virtual reality (VR) environment positively and enjoyed the interactions they had with international interlocutors via VR technologies.

Barrot (2022) reviewed the literature on social media published between 2008 and 2019 and reported that social media platforms such as *Facebook*, *Skype*, and *Twitter* attracted great attention from language learning scholars due to "their multiple and flexible communication affordances, wide geographical distribution, and large number of active users" (p. 2557). In a review of academic literature on the use of digital technology in education, Taylor et al. (2021) stated that "digital learning activities, which promote purposeful communication and collaboration amongst teachers and students, open greater opportunities to converse in creative and meaningful ways when compared to non-digital learning activities" (p. 4). They also said, "Integrating communicative digital tools, into classroom practice such as *Facebook* and discussion forums, can support core learning areas and digital literacy across subjects, foster 21st century skills, and cultivate cultural awareness and digital citizenship" (p. 4). For the effective implementation of digital communication activities in the language classroom, it is necessary to address potential challenges such as technical barriers and security concerns. Teachers need to find ways of overcoming the challenges and offering students positive and impactful language learning experiences through right communication channels and well-planned activities.

Task 4.1

Explore ways of communicating in digital environments and discuss what digital communication activities can be used in the language classroom.

4.2 Developing digital communication skills

It is important for language learners to be aware of differences in cultural, social, professional, and personal norms when communicating with people from different backgrounds. They need to create positive connections with others and develop digital communication strategies to participate in authentic networks online. Godwin-Jones (2015) said, "Participating in emerging online communities may require users to develop new skills, acquire specific software or hardware, and/or learn particular conventions and behavior norms" (p. 8). He discussed how language learners achieve literacy gains through participation in online communities and emphasised the need for learner training, which empowers language learning with online tools and resources. He suggested the use of learner diaries, logs, or portfolios as a valuable approach to reflect on the process of language learning with digital tools and services. We can try and evaluate the tools and services to see how they improve our digital communication.

Warnecke and Lominé (2011) provided the following guidelines for planning and designing tasks to facilitate interaction in online sessions:

- Be aware that tasks tend to take longer than in face-to-face settings.
- The best session plan often includes a move from highly structured and closed tasks to more creative and open-ended ones.
- Employing too many different tools during one online session may be confusing for participants; using fewer tools keeps the focus on interaction in the language rather than on mastering the technology.
- Using and modifying a limited number of materials during a session tends to be beneficial for time management.
- Visuals may support interaction, but they need to be carefully tailored. Showing video clips in the L2 can have a disheartening effect if the level of the language spoken is too complex for the group.
- Each task should have a clearly defined beginning and end, with outcomes that can be visualised by the learners.
- Time planning for tasks needs to take account of extra time needed for managing screens, moving between rooms or using interactive features. (pp. 138–139)

They also suggested the following task types for online synchronous sessions: "brainstorming; role-play; dialogues; working with visual images; reviewing core vocabulary; information gap or 'jigsaw' tasks; and storytelling and retelling" (p. 139). These task types can be considered when teachers design open-ended tasks offering creative and meaningful learning experiences in digital communication.

Example activities for developing digital communication skills in the language classroom are given below.

Activity 4.1

Online discussion forums

Introduction	This activity gives students opportunities to engage in online discussions in the form of posted messages in their target language. It facilitates interactive asynchronous communication among students.
Target Language	Any language
Target Language Skills & Areas	Reading, writing, vocabulary, and grammar
Learner Levels	All levels
Activity Length	30–50 minutes
Preparation Time	30–50 minutes
Technical Requirements & Resources	A computer for each student
	An online discussion platform such as *Kialo Edu* (https://www.kialo-edu.com/) or *Parlay* (https://parlayideas.com/); or open source forum software such as *MyBB* (https://mybb.com/) or *phpBB* (https://www.phpbb.com/)
	Topic selection resources: web search engines such as *Google* (https://www.google.com/) and *Bing* (https://www.bing.com/); or video sharing tools such as *YouTube* (https://www.youtube.com/) and *SchoolTube* (https://schooltube.com/)
Procedure	1. Choose a discussion topic or question that is meaningful to students.
2. Assign the students to participate in an online discussion on the selected topic.
3. Guide the students to communicate effectively and consider different views.
4. Ask the students to support their arguments with evidence or references.
5. Encourage the students to make comments on other students' posts.
6. Moderate the students' discussion whenever needed.
7. Invite the students to discuss their experience with the online discussion.

Continued....

Activity 4.1 *Continued....*

Options and Suggestions	• The teacher can consider allowing students to discuss a topic of their choice. • The teacher can guide students to include and use relevant multimedia resources in their posts.

Activity 4.2

Video conferencing

Introduction	This activity is designed to increase students' online engagement and improve their listening and speaking skills in a video conferencing environment.
Target Language	Any language
Target Language Skills & Areas	Listening and speaking
Learner Levels	All levels
Activity Length	30–50 minutes
Preparation Time	30–50 minutes
Technical Requirements & Resources	A computer for each student or each group A video communication platform such as *Skype* (https://www.skype.com/) or *Zoom* (https://zoom.us/) *Padlet* (https://padlet.com/)
Procedure	1. Teach students how to use a video conferencing tool. 2. Invite the students to participate in a video conference with their classmates or a guest speaker. 3. Give the students instructions on what they need to do. 4. Guide the students communicate effectively and ask questions in an appropriate manner. 5. Encourage the students to post their questions or opinions to *Padlet* during the synchronous session. 6. Check and follow up the students' posts on *Padlet*. 7. Have a discussion on the topic of the video conference and summarise it.
Options and Suggestions	• The teacher can consider using breakout rooms for small groups during the video conference when needed. • The teacher can assign students to give virtual presentations as a part of the video conference activity.

Activity 4.3

Digital storytelling

Introduction	This activity is designed for students to create and share their stories by presenting their multimedia production online. It involves combining various digital media (e.g., text, images, audio, videos) within a story and creates engaging and immersive experiences for students.
Target Language	Any language
Target Language Skills & Areas	Reading, writing, listening, and speaking
Learner Levels	All levels
Activity Length	40–60 minutes
Preparation Time	40–60 minutes
Technical Requirements & Resources	A computer for each student or each group Digital storytelling creation tools such as *FlowVella* (https://flowvella.com/), *Pixton* (https://www.pixton.com/), *Storybird* (https://storybird.com/), *StoryboardThat* (https://www.storyboardthat.com/), and *ThingLink* (https://www.thinglink.com/)
Procedure	1. Introduce a digital storytelling creation tool to students. 2. Assign the students a task to create a digital story in the format of an interactive presentation or a video. 3. Guide the students to understand what they need to do and how they can do it. 4. Encourage the students to communicate their story clearly and use multimedia to support their story. 5. Check the students' progress and give guidance and feedback whenever needed. 6. Ask the students to submit and present their work. 7. Have a group discussion about what the students learnt from the activity.
Options and Suggestions	• Teachers are encouraged to explore a range of digital tools that can be used for the activity. • Teachers can choose different learning styles and preferences to enhance students' attention and participation.

Activity 4.4

Online role play

Introduction	This activity gives students opportunities to assume the role of another person and perform the character of the person in a given situation. It enables students to experience examples of language practices, behaviours, and decision-making skills.
Target Language	Any language
Target Language Skills & Areas	Reading, writing, listening, and speaking
Learner Levels	Intermediate to advanced levels
Activity Length	30–50 minutes
Preparation Time	30–50 minutes
Technical Requirements & Resources	A computer for each student or each group A video conferencing platform (e.g., *Zoom* [https://zoom.us/]); an online text-based roleplaying community (e.g., *RolePlayer.me* [https://www.roleplay.me]); or an online multimedia platform [e.g., *Second Life* (https://secondlife.com/])
Procedure	1. Introduce a digital platform to be used for the activity. 2. Assign the students a task to participate in an online role play (e.g., interviewing, marketing, negotiating, counselling, debating). 3. Explain the purpose of the role play and how the role play will be assessed. 4. Guide the students to understand what they need to do and how they can do it. 5. Allow time for the students to practice the role play. 6. Encourage the students to communicate appropriately, consider different perspectives, and use digital tools to support their role. 7. Have a group discussion about what the students learnt from the activity.
Options and Suggestions	• The teacher can use scenarios relevant to real-world situations. • The teacher can encourage critical observation of peers in the role play.

Additional Activities

The following example activity (Son, 2023b) shows how a digital communication activity can be implemented with a videoconferencing tool.

Activity Title	Tracking understanding and learning in video conferencing
Introduction	The use of videoconferencing tools such as *Skype* (https://www.skype.com/) and *Zoom* (https://zoom.us/) has become essential in online language teaching. This activity gives learners an opportunity to improve their listening and speaking skills in a *Zoom* environment.
Target Language	Any language
Target Language Skills & Areas	Listening and speaking
Learner Levels	All levels
Activity Aims	This activity aims to increase learners' online engagement by using *Zoom* and live polls.
Activity Length	30 minutes
Preparation Time	30 minutes
Technical Requirements & Resources	*Zoom* (https://zoom.us/); *Mentimeter* (https://www.mentimeter.com/)
Procedure	1. Give an introduction to all participants in *Zoom* (https://zoom.us/). 2. Log in *Mentimeter* (https://www.mentimeter.com/) and present a question containing target words to learn in Present Mode. 3. Share the screen showing the question with the participants in *Zoom*. 4. Invite the participants to go to https://www.menti.com/ and enter the given code. 5. Ask the participants to submit their choices. 6. Check the number of votes in a live presentation. 7. Discuss the results of the votes in the whole group and/or small groups in break-out rooms. 8. Summarise the *Zoom* session.
Options and Suggestions	• Language teaching with *Zoom* comes with various educational concerns. One of the concerns is the design and implementation of online activities.

Continued....

Additional Activities *Continued....*

	• Other videoconferencing activities teachers can consider include: delivering oral presentations on specific topics appropriate and interesting to learners; playing roles in a scenario or debate; and taking quizzes with *Kahoot!* (https://kahoot.com/) or *Quizlet* (https://quizlet.com/).
Justification	There has been a shift from traditional classroom teaching to online teaching due to the global COVID-19 pandemic. The shift has posed significant challenges for language teachers and learners. In online language teaching, synchronous communication is commonly used (Peachey, 2017). Many language teachers utilise videoconferencing tools such as *Zoom* to deliver live sessions (Moorhouse & Beaumont, 2020). *Zoom* offers several features such as annotation tools, polls, breakout rooms, and sharing screens (Kohnke & Moorhouse, 2022). In order to facilitate active language learning, *Zoom* can be combined with other additional tools such as audience response systems (e.g., *Mentimeter, GoSoapBox*), game-based learning platforms (e.g., *Kahoot!, Quizlet*), and/or word clouds (e.g., *MonkeyLearn, Tagxedo*). It is important to use the features of these online tools appropriately within a sequence of learning in each lesson (Moorhouse & Beaumont, 2020). Language teachers are encouraged to develop their competence in online language teaching and videoconferencing teaching strategies.
References and Further Reading	Kohnke, L., & Moorhouse, B. L. (2022). Facilitating synchronous online language learning through Zoom. *RELC Journal, 53*(1), 296-301. https://doi.org/10.1177/0033688220937235 Moorhouse, B. L., & Beaumont, A. M. (2020). Utilizing video conferencing software to teach young language learners in Hong Kong during the COVID-19 class suspensions. *TESOL Journal, 11*(3), e00545. https://doi.org/10.1002/tesj.545 Peachey, N. (2017). Synchronous online teaching. In M. Carrier, R. M. Damerow, & K. M. Bailey (Eds.), *Digital language learning and teaching: Research, theory, and practice* (pp. 143–155). Routledge.

Continued....

Additional Activities *Continued....*

>   Son, J.-B. (2010). Online tools for language teaching.
>   https://drjbson.com/projects/tools/
>   Son, J.-B. (2015). Digital literacy. https://drjbson.com/projects/dl/
>   Son, J.-B. (2017). Online activities for language learning.
>   https://drjbson.com/projects/oall/
>
>   (Son, 2023b, pp. 3–5)

The following example activity (Alm, 2020) demonstrates the use of a chat app for a digital communication activity.

Activity Title	L2 chat for semi-formal and informal language learning
Introduction	L2 chat is a widely researched area in formal language learning settings, primarily focusing on aspects of language development (Sauro, 2012). This activity offers a semi-formal approach, supporting language learners to self-initiate L2 chat between peers and with native speakers.
Target Language	Any language
Target Language Skills & Areas	Conversational practice, chatting
Learner Levels	Intermediate adult learners
Activity Aims	This activity aims to extend L2 practice of language learners by involving them in semi-formal chat activities using a chat app. The term semi-formal emphasises the focus on self-initiation, both in task involvement and task performance. The activity is assigned in a formal space (the language class) and performed in the private space of the learner. Students are asked to initiate a chat about a topic of their choice, with self-selected chat partners (from their class), and to conduct the chat in their own time. Students learn to engage with others through chat and to maintain one or several chat threads. The activity also aims to prepare students for subsequent informal engagement with native speakers on the same app.
Activity Length	20–30 minutes per chat (suggested time)
Preparation Time	Installation of app and setting up of profiles: 5 minutes Training session: 15 minutes Preparation of chat session by students: 60 minutes

Continued....

Technical Requirements & Resources	*HelloTalk* (https://www.hellotalk.com) app (iOS, Android) free
	HelloTalk is an L2 chat app that allows native speakers and language learners to engage in co-constructive L2 language exchanges. Similar apps, such as *Bilingua* (https://bilingua.io) could be used, but *HelloTalk* has the advantage of having group functions. Having gained confidence through using the app with their classmates, learners are prepared to engage informally in language exchange with conversation partners selected from the app.
Procedure	**Technical procedures** 1. Download *HelloTalk*. 2. Students set up their individual profiles. 3. Teacher sets up a group for all students of the class. **Technical training** Students are given an overview of: 1. language-related chat functions (e.g., translation and correction tools) 2. functional features (e.g., direct reply) 3. the language partner matching function (in preparation for subsequent informal chat practice) **Task instruction** To prepare for their chat moderation, students need to: 1. decide on a topic (e.g., hobbies, shopping, music) 2. look up relevant vocabulary 3. prepare a minimum of five questions During the chat, they need to keep the conversation going by: 1. asking questions that prompt others to participate 2. responding appropriately to messages After approximately 20 minutes, the designated moderator concludes the chat by thanking everybody for their participation. Once the chat is completed, the teacher has access to the transcript of the conversation.
Options and Suggestions	• To use this app confidently with their students, teachers should familiarise themselves with the app, ideally by taking a learner perspective and engaging in some chats with informal language learners from the *HelloTalk* community.

Continued....

- The teacher has the option of actively participating in the chats, observing without interfering, or alternatively staying out of the conversation.
- One could build in a focus on accuracy and ask students to correct each other with the correction tool.
- Using the "favourite" tool, students can be asked to create a list of idiomatic phrases they encounter during their chats.
- Further, the app also has voice and video recording options, allowing multimodal and creative L2 use.
- Students can be encouraged to keep interacting with each other beyond the assigned activity and to seek additional language partners on the app.
- Students should be made aware about privacy issues, as well as cyber bulling and harassing that might occur when engaging with self-selected tandem partners in an unmonitored learning environment. For this reason, the activity is only recommended for adult learners.

Justification	This activity supports the development of learners' confidence and ability to engage in L2 chat as well as their conversational language skills. Theories in educational psychology (McCombs, 1991) have long shown that activation of personal interest and a sense of responsibility for the learning situation can have a positive effect on task engagement. In this semi-formal activity, students are put in charge of their conversation topic (personal interest) and of the moderation of the group chat (responsibility), supporting this imperative. Text chat or written synchronous computer-mediated communication (SCMC) is highly relevant for language learners as it is a pervasive means of communication. Two decades of SCMC research have established text chat as "an acknowledged context for L2 practice and development" (Michel, 2018, p. 164). Its similarity to spoken language (e.g., short turns, informal language), yet slower pace in turn-taking, enables language learners to practice their language skills as it prepares them for realistic spoken and written chat communications. In this activity, students take turns as chat moderators. In this role, they are required to anticipate questions and responses around the chosen topic (similar to the use

Continued....

of language strategies to prepare for spoken interaction, cf. Cohen, 1996). As they use these rehearsed phrases in the chat, they apply their prepared work in a semi-formal context, receiving immediate feedback from their peers. This process prepares students for subsequent conversations in less structured and more spontaneous chats with self-selected chat partners through the app.

References and Further Reading

Cohen, A. D. (1996). *Second language learning and use strategies: Clarifying the issues*. Center for Advanced Research on Language, University of Minnesota.

McCombs, B. L. (1991). Motivation and lifelong learning. *Educational Psychologist, 26*(2), 117–127.

Michel, M. (2018). Practising online with your peers: The role of text chat for second language development. In C. Jones (Ed.), *Practice in second language learning* (pp. 164–196). Cambridge University Press.

Nushi, M., & Makiabadi, H. (2018). HelloTalk: A language exchange app on your smartphone. *Roshd Journal of Foreign Language Teaching, 33*(2), 16–23.

Sauro, S. (2012). L2 performance in text-chat and spoken discourse. *System, 40*(3), 335-348. https://doi.org/10.1016/j.system.2012.08.001

Vollmer Rivera, A. (2017). HelloTalk. *CALICO Journal, 34*(3), 384-392. https://doi.org/10.1558/cj.32432

(Alm, 2020, pp. 38–41)

Task 4.2a

Discuss what digital communication strategies could be used in intercultural situations.

Task 4.2b

Discuss what digital communication activities could be useful for developing intercultural competence.

Discussion Questions

1. What digital tools do you use to communicate online?
2. What social rules or customs do you use in digital communication?
3. What do you think students need to know to communicate in the world that is multimodal and multilingual?
4. How can you support students' meaning-making in digital environments?
5. How can you help students be active, effective, and reflective in digital communication?
6. What sorts of critical questioning might you need to support students to engage effectively in digital communication?
7. What is the role of communication in digital language teacher development?
8. What skills and strategies do language teachers and students need to develop for effective digital communication?
9. How can teachers help students improve their understanding of how digital technologies can support communication for particular audiences?
10. How can teachers provide students with authentic opportunities to develop digital communication skills in the classroom and out of the classroom?

5
Collaboration

Digital collaboration involves using digital technologies to collaborate with others. It connects a broad network of individuals across different locations and time zones. It requires digital communication and interaction and can lead to increased understanding and productivity. Digital collaboration tools include collaborative real-time editing tools (e.g., *ClickUp* [https://clickup.com/], *Etherpad* [https://etherpad.org/], *Google Docs* [https://docs.google.com/]), social bookmarking tools (e.g., *Diigo* [https://www.diigo.com/], *Pinterest* [https://www.pinterest.com/]), collaborative diagramming tools (e.g., *Cacoo* [https://cacoo.com/], *Creately* [https://creately.com/]), virtual communities (e.g., *Busuu* [https://www.busuu.com/], *italki* [https://www.italki.com/]), and wikis (e.g., *PBworks* [https://www.pbworks.com/wikis.html], *SlimWiki* [https://slimwiki.com/], *Wikidot* [https://www.wikidot.com/]). The ability to participate in digital collaboration effectively is needed for cooperation, teamwork, problem-solving, and respect for diversity. It enables language learners to engage in collaborative learning and work on dynamic group projects. It also helps them build their confidence and fluency in their target language and increase their intercultural understanding and communication skills. This chapter explores digital collaboration and discusses how to develop digital collaboration skills in the context of language learning and teaching.

5.1 Collaborating online

Digital collaboration is the process of working with others online. It allows us to work with others no matter where we are. Albert et al. (2009) commented:

> Information and communication technologies now allow the human community to reach into the past for archival knowledge and to reach into the future to make plans for what has not yet happened. Communication networks, along with the ICT tools of modern societies, are the outward expressions of society's aspirations to learn about others, to engage in trade and to collaborate at a distance. (p. 5)

Regarding collaboration in learning and teaching, Hammond (2017) stated, "Collaboration is crucial to learning because it is through effort of explaining and defending positions, exploring differences and reaching agreement, that new knowledge is created" (p. 1011). He posited that "the case for cooperation and collaboration is based upon an idea that having students work together will lead to more positive learning outcomes and more engaged learners" and added, "This is because there are processes in collaboration which make an identifiable contribution to learning and may be considered as learning in their own right. Collaboration offers a more relevant experience for learners and one that chimes better with the contemporary world; the relentless focus on individual achievement is not the natural way of learning but an early modernist aberration" (p. 1019). In a comparison between the traditional view of collaboration and online collaboration, he said, "Online collaboration, it is argued, involves a change of environment for learners with consequences in particular for reach, media and archiving of interaction. However, OC should be seen as an evolution of a tradition rather than a paradigm shift in teaching and learning" (p. 1019).

Hague and Payton (2010) stated, "When students participate in collaborative group work, they need to be able to explain their ideas and enter into negotiations when those ideas do not align with others in the group. Learning how to collaborate can therefore also help students to develop skills of debate, flexibility, cooperation, compromise and listening" (p. 28). They also remarked, "Teachers can facilitate effective group work by supporting students to develop strategies for making collaboration easier" (p. 30). Similarly, Payton and Hague (2010) stated: "The ability to collaborate is to work successfully with others to co-create meaning and knowledge. Supporting young people's digital literacy involves developing their understanding of how meanings are collaboratively created using digital technologies and how digital technologies (for example, shared documents such as wikis) can effectively support collaborative processes within the classroom and with wider world" (p. 61). In this way, collaborative problem-solving is possible in digital environments.

The Australian Curriculum, Assessment and Reporting Authority (ACARA) (2021) specified that, through collaborating online, "students develop the capacity to interact and collaborate with an online community of peers and experts for the construction and co-creation of knowledge" (p. 8). In collaborating through digital channels, students need positive attitudes to be "willing to share and collaborate with others", be "ready to function as part of a team", and look for "new forms of collaboration that are not necessarily based on a previous face-to-face engagement" (Ferrari, 2013, p. 23). With a focus on online language teaching, Stickler (2022) pointed out that, considering socio-cultural learning theories, "the importance of others in the learning environment immediately becomes clear" and it "leads to collaboration and group work as important features of the online classroom" (p. 18).

Digital networks support student collaboration within and beyond the classroom. As mentioned by Lotherington and Ronda (2014), digital media offer opportunities for global collaboration. They said, "New digital competencies essentially include collaboration, with social, gaming, and professional platforms offering different patterns of working together. The concept of expert knowledge is no longer equated with individual knowledge" (p. 18). They also noted:

> Collaborative work can be facilitated through peer sharing and peer feedback, collaborative composition and media creation, and participation in virtual class discussions. More important, collaboration can happen outside the classroom with the wider community of users in the production of digital content, allowing learners to engage with cutting-edge digital media and make a contribution to a current event. (p. 22)

Language learners and teachers can expand their networks, share their ideas and knowledge, and participate in online communities of practice by collaborating through digital technologies. They can take part in collaborative online environments (e.g., blogs, wikis, webinars, online discussion forums, online meetings, social media groups) and share digital resources (e.g., text documents, website links, images, presentations) with people from different cultural and language backgrounds. In foreign language education, online intercultural collaboration is evidently shown in telecollaboration (or virtual exchange), which has grown dramatically in the last three decades (O'Dowd & O'Rourke, 2019). Telecollaboration involves working with people from different cultural backgrounds and demonstrates the interactive nature of digital literacy (Kern, 2021).

Aoki and Molnar (2011) asserted that language learners' understanding of cultural concepts and attitudes becomes more contextualised when they participate in the process of communication and collaboration with people in the target culture. In a study of project-based collaborative learning in telecollaboration between two university classes in Hungary and Japan, they utilised *Facebook* (https://www.facebook.com/), *Skype* (https://www.skype.com/), *Google Docs* (https://docs.google.com), and *VoiceThread* (https://voicethread.com/) and found issues with communication breakdowns between the two groups and relying on asynchronous means of communication due to time differences. They concluded that the telecollaboration gave the students actual opportunities to use the digital tools although there were challenges to improve the students' interpersonal and intercultural communication skills and time management skills.

In a systematic review of research on technology-enhanced collaborative language learning in which teachers design technology-supported collaborative tasks and learners complete the assigned tasks in groups or pairs, Su and Zou (2022) reported that both task design and students' technology knowledge placed great influences on the effectiveness of collaborative language learning. They highlighted that "digital literacy is a prerequisite of adept utilization of language learning technology" and argued that "coordination between language and technology teachers is necessary for removal of technical barriers and quality assurance" (p. 1773). They proposed technologies for collaborative language learning shown in Table 5.1.

In language teacher development, collaboration is strongly encouraged. Through participation in online communities of practice or online teacher networks (Son, 2014a), teachers can collaborate with colleagues locally, nationally, and internationally. Collaboration is one of the four elements of Son's (2018) teacher development model, which incorporates exploration, communication, collaboration, and reflection (ECCR). He encouraged teachers "to get involved in collaborative knowledge building and sharing" (p. 61). In an earlier study (Son, 2006), he confirmed that the use of CMC for collaboration allowed teachers to have collaborative learning channels for sharing ideas and resources with their fellow teachers. His findings highlighted the interrelationships between digital communication and digital collaboration.

Task 5.1

We live and work in networked communities and use digital technologies for online interaction and collaboration in the communities. Share your experience with digital collaboration in your professional community.

Table 5.1 *Collaborative Language Learning Technologies (adapted from Su & Zou, 2022, pp. 1787–1788)*

Language skill and knowledge	Technology	Student activity	Teacher activity
Speaking	3D Multi-User Virtual World (3DVW)	• exchanging information by speaking with partners to collaboratively pass the final test in the virtual world	• explaining the use of technology and learning objectives
	MyET	• identifying partners' pronunciation problems when they verbally read the articles • correcting each other's weakness according to the automatic feedback	• organizing staged collaborative activities • supervising and checking the collaboration process
	Single-display Groupware (SDG)	• co-learning and co-acting in front of the shared screen • correcting partners' pronunciation errors • sharing ideas through audio, video, or messages	• reducing group conflicts • assigning tasks for each group member • offering assistance when necessary
	Skype	• communicating with partners on unclear knowledge or negotiating disagreements	• giving progressive feedback
Listening	3D Multi-User Virtual World (3DVW) Single-display Groupware (SDG)	• students exchange prompts based on some of the pre-recorded conversations that they listened to • students co-organize the information that they listened to in sequence	• correcting students' errors

Skill	Tool	Activities
Reading	Moodle	• doing assignments according to the reading • sharing articles and co-discussing the reading contents via discussion forum • offering feedback
	3D Multi-User Virtual World (3DVW)	• individually read specific written information attached to 3D objects in the virtual world • exchanging detailed and useful information
Writing	Google Docs	• online co-writing, co-editing, and co-finalization
	Twitter	• online discussion and idea sharing
	Blogging	• exchanging ideas through posts, comments, and re-sending others' posts with comments • giving a like to the posting or comment
Vocabulary	WhatsApp	• practicing vocabulary knowledge with group mates anytime and anywhere • co-describing and co-defining words'
	Vine	• visual associations to link the target words together
Problem-solving and reasoning skills	Digital Mysteries	• exchanging different digital cues, co-analyzing the problem-solving solutions, and co-discussing the solutions to co-answer the exploratory questions

5.2 Developing digital collaboration skills

Developing digital collaboration skills is critical in language learning and teaching. Teachers need to provide students with opportunities and resources to collaborate in digital formats and develop both digital literacy and language skills. They can teach digital collaboration skills through digital collaboration activities in language lessons. For example, Lankshear and Knobel (2006) suggested fanfiction (e.g., *FanFiction.net* [https://www.fanfiction.net/]) as a collaborative writing activity and pointed out that "fanfiction writing online is often a highly collaborative act" (p. 16). Taking a different approach, Payton and Hague (2010) suggested a wiki activity using *PBWorks* (https://www.pbworks.com/wikis.html) as wikis offer "collaborative online spaces" and encourage "collaborative collation of information and creation of text" (p. 30).

More detailed example activities for developing digital collaboration skills are given below.

Activity 5.1

Online group project

Introduction	This activity is designed to help students learn from collective work on an online group project. It encourages students to communicate and collaborate actively with their group members, consider others' perspectives, use digital tools, and make a group decision to produce and present a final product.
Target Language	Any language
Target Language Skills & Areas	Reading, writing, listening, and speaking
Learner Levels	Intermediate to advanced levels
Activity Length	40–60 minutes
Preparation Time	40–60 minutes
Technical Requirements & Resources	A computer for each student or each group
	A mind mapping tool such as *Mindmeister* (https://www.mindmeister.com/) or *Mindomo* (https://www.mindomo.com/)
	A virtual wall such as *Padlet* (https://padlet.com/) or *Netboard.me* (https://netboard.me/)

Continued....

Activity 5.1 *Continued....*

	Web search engines such as *Google* (https://www.google.com/) and *Bing* (https://www.bing.com/)
	Free image hosting sites such as *Google Photos* (https://photos.google.com/), *Pexels* (https://www.pexels.com/), *Pixabay* (https://pixabay.com/), and *Unsplash* (https://unsplash.com/)
	A digital audio editors such as *Audacity* (https://www.audacityteam.org/) or *Ocenaudio* (https://www.ocenaudio.com/)
Procedure	1. Divide the class into groups of three or four students.
	2. Assign the students a task (e.g., undertaking a research project into a particular topic, creating a collection of images representing a specific word, making a podcast) to work on a group project online.
	3. Guide the students to communicate effectively and use digital tools and resources properly.
	4. Encourage the students to collaborate and make a group decision.
	5. Ask the students to present their report or product online.
	6. Give feedback on each report or product.
	7. Invite the students to discuss their experience with the group project.
Options and Suggestions	• The teacher can consider a variety of project tasks, topics, and research questions.
	• The teacher can guide students to include and use relevant multimedia resources in their product.

Activity 5.2

Collaborative writing

Introduction	This activity is designed for students to work together on a collaborative writing task (e.g., a group blog post, a wiki page). It facilitates writing development and constructive interactions with peers.
Target Language	Any language
Target Language Skills & Areas	Writing

Continued....

Activity 5.2 *Continued....*

Learner Levels	All levels
Activity Length	30–50 minutes
Preparation Time	30–50 minutes
Technical Requirements & Resources	A computer for each student or each group
	A blogging platform such as *Blogger* (https://www.blogger.com/), *Edublogs* (https://edublogs.org/), or *WordPress* (https://wordpress.com/)
	A wiki service such as *PBworks* (https://www.pbworks.com/wikis.html), *SlimWiki* (https://slimwiki.com/), or *Wikidot* (https://www.wikidot.com/)
Procedure	1. Divide the class into groups of three or four students.
	2. Assign the students a group writing task to collaborate online in the format of a blog or a wiki.
	3. Give the students instructions on what they need to do and how they can do it.
	4. Guide the students to communicate effectively and use digital tools and resources in a reasonable manner.
	5. Encourage the students to collaborate in writing, revising, and reviewing and make a group decision.
	6. Ask the students to present their blog post or wiki page.
	7. Give feedback on each post or page.
	8. Invite the students to discuss their experience with the collaborative writing.
Options and Suggestions	• The teacher can consider a variety of topics students can write about.
	• The teacher can collate and present what all groups write online through a website or a virtual wall for further exploration.

Activity 5.3

Virtual brainstorming

Introduction	This activity gives students opportunities to come up with thoughts and ideas and discuss them in a group online. It allows group members to generate ideas and participate in group discussions online for a group project.

Continued....

Activity 5.3 *Continued....*

Target Language	Any language
Target Language Skills & Areas	Listening and speaking
Learner Levels	All levels
Activity Length	30–50 minutes
Preparation Time	30–50 minutes
Technical Requirements & Resources	A computer for each student or each group
	A mind mapping tool such as *Mindmeister* (https://www.mindmeister.com/) or *Mindomo* (https://www.mindomo.com/)
	A video communication platform such as *Skype* (https://www.skype.com/) or *Zoom* (https://zoom.us/)
	An online whiteboard such as *Zoom Whiteboard* (https://explore.zoom.us/en/products/online-whiteboard/), *Microsoft Whiteboard* (https://www.microsoft.com/en-au/microsoft-365/microsoft-whiteboard/), *Miro* (https://miro.com/), or *Mural* (https://mural.co/)
Procedure	1. Divide the class into groups of three or four students.
	2. Assign the students a group task to discuss online (e.g., a mind mapping tool, a video communication platform, an online whiteboard).
	3. Give the students instructions on what they need to do and how they can do it.
	4. Guide the students to communicate effectively and use digital tools and resources when needed.
	5. Encourage the students to collaborate to propose ideas and suggestions.
	6. Check the students' progress and give guidance and feedback whenever needed.
	7. Ask each group to present their ideas and suggestions.
	8. Invite the students to discuss their experience with the virtual brainstorming.
Options and Suggestions	• The teacher can consider a variety of topics, issues, and questions that students can discuss online.
	• The teacher can collate and present all outcomes online through a website or a virtual wall for further discussion.

Continued....

Activity 5.4

Virtual team building

Introduction	This activity gives students opportunities to create connections between team members online. It helps improve collaboration skills, foster teamwork, and increase group productivity.
Target Language	Any language
Target Language Skills & Areas	Reading, writing, listening, and speaking
Learner Levels	Intermediate to advanced levels
Activity Length	30–50 minutes
Preparation Time	30–50 minutes
Technical Requirements & Resources	A computer for each student or each group
	A video conferencing platform such as *Skype* (https://www.skype.com/) or *Zoom* (https://zoom.us/)
	An educational game creation tool such as *Kahoot!* (https://kahoot.com/) or *Quizlet* (https://quizlet.com/)
	A jigsaw puzzle maker such as *Jigsaw Planet* (https://www.jigsawplanet.com/), *Daily Jigsaw Puzzles* (https://www.dailyjigsawpuzzles.net/puzzle-maker.html), or *Jigidi* (https://www.jigidi.com/)
Procedure	1. Create a virtual team building activity (e.g., icebreaker questions, an online game, an online puzzle, an online event planner, a virtual book club).
	2. Give students instructions on how to participate in the activity and what they need to do.
	3. Guide the students to collaborate and communicate effectively.
	4. Encourage the students to work together to achieve the goal of the activity.
	5. Allow time for the students to complete the activity.
	6. Give guidance and feedback whenever needed.
	7. Have a group discussion about what the students learnt from the activity.
Options and Suggestions	• The teacher can consider using various types of online games for this activity.
	• The teacher can empathise social interactions among participants throughout the activity.

Additional Activities

The following example activity (Campbell, 2023) shows how a digital collaboration activity can be used for grammar and spoken practice.

Activity Title	Using digitally shared student-generated questions
Introduction	This activity is a versatile, student-centered, computer-assisted writing and speaking activity, usable at most levels and on unlimited topics (e.g., food & drink, climate crisis, summer plans), which provides a rich opportunity to focus on grammatical accuracy and practice conversation.
Target Language	Various languages including English
Target Language Skills & Areas	Writing, speaking, pronunciation and grammar
Learner Levels	Common European Framework of References for Languages (CEFR) A2 to C2
Activity Aims	This activity aims to help students learn or review various items of grammar through production of written questions and error correction. It offers an opportunity to internalize corrected forms through spoken practice.
Activity Length	20–30 minutes (divided into two parts, typically positioned before and after a separate listening or reading comprehension activity on an identical or related topic, thereby giving the teacher the time to make corrections by the computer)
Preparation Time	10 minutes (for setting up)
Technical Requirements & Resources	A computer or a smartphone with access to a word processor and a class blog or chat space; *Google Docs* (https://docs.google.com/); *Blogger* (https://www.blogger.com/); *Zoom* (https://zoom.us/); *Quizlet* (https://quizlet.com/); *Vocaroo* (https://vocaroo.com/); *ZenGengo* (https://www.zengengo.com/)
Procedure	1. Either individually or in pairs, using *Google Docs* (https://docs.google.com/), students write their own original questions (three to five) related to the lesson's topic, which they can use later for pair-work speaking practice (e.g, What is your least favourite food? How can we reduce global warming? What are you planning to do during the vacation?).

Continued....

Additional Activities *Continued....*

2. The students copy and paste these questions (with names shown or anonymously) into *Blogger* (https://www.blogger.com/) or *Zoom Chat* (https://explore.zoom.us/en/products/group-chat/).
3. The students then engage in a separate activity, normally listening or reading comprehension, on a related topic. While they are occupied with this, the teacher has the chance to check their questions for grammatical or other errors and add some new questions if needed.
4. When ready, the teacher shows a selection of any incorrect questions on the classroom display and guides the students towards correcting them. Phonological practice is recommended here. Finally, the teacher uploads the full list of corrected questions to *Blogger* or *Zoom Chat*, which the students use in the following stage.
5. The students work in pairs or small groups and carry out question-answer-reaction-follow-up question (QARF) speaking practice using some or all of the corrected question list.

Options and Suggestions

- If students stick just to writing safe and simple questions, the teacher can add some supplementary questions in order to expand their awareness of more complex issues as well as more advanced vocabulary or structures.
- The teacher helps those students requiring extra support during speaking practice (Stage 5 of the Procedure).
- To provide a greater cognitive challenge, the teacher can upload the corrected text as "dehydrated" questions (e.g., What / you / have / breakfast / today?), which act as a scaffold.
- During the speaking activity, students are encouraged to employ some of the new language they encountered in their separate comprehension activity (Stage 3).

Continued....

Chapter 5

Additional Activities *Continued....*

	- Students are asked to select, copy, and paste some of the corrected questions into their *Quizlet* (https://quizlet.com/) vocabulary sets before they forget them.
- As an audio aide-mémoire, students can record and keep full conversations or just answers, for example, using *Vocaroo* (https://vocaroo.com/).
- These mp3s can also be submitted to the teacher for evaluation using *Google Forms* (https://docs.google.com/forms), *ZenGengo* (https://www.zengengo.com/), email, etc.
- To provide a more advanced model (in terms of content, language, and phonology) for students to compare with their own attempts, the teacher can record and upload sample audio answers to the same questions.
Justification	Inviting students to supply their own questions belongs to a student-centred, active learning approach (Laurillard, 2012) and has been investigated for L2 learning (Song, et al., 2017). Tomlinson and Masuhara (2018) argue that, ideally, a course should contain principled selections from various textbooks, supplemented by materials made not only by the teacher but also by the students. Allowing them to create original content for communication can lead to a more meaningful and motivating activity based on their authentic concerns. This move away from textbook-based materials is also a key component of the Dogme ELT approach (Meddings & Thornbury, 2015) in which the "content most likely to engage learners and to trigger learning processes is that which is already there, supplied by the people in the room" (p. 7). The pedagogy is materials-light and conversation-driven with a focus on emergent language rather than on whatever happens to appear next in the textbook.

Continued....

Additional Activities *Continued....*

Opportunities for collaborative explicit error correction (form, spelling, phonology) are numerous and may have a durable effect on learning, especially, as Ellis (2012) points out, since instruction is embedded in communicative activities. Williams and Evans (1998) emphasize, however, that the complexity of the forms in question will affect the outcome. It is intended that students can automatize their linguistic knowledge thanks to repeated production of written and spoken language in the final two stages of the activity (Ellis, 2003; Swain, 1985).

References and Further Reading

Ellis, R. (2003). *Task-based language learning and teaching.* Oxford University Press.

Ellis, R. (2012). *Language teaching research and language pedagogy.* Wiley-Blackwell.

Laurillard, D. (2012). *Teaching as a design science.* Routledge.

Meddings, L., & Thornbury, S. (2015). *Teaching unplugged: Dogme in English language teaching.* Delta Publishing.

Song, D., Oh, E.Y., & Glazewski, K. (2017). Student-generated questioning activity in second language courses using a customized personal response system: A case study. *Educational Technology Research and Development, 65,* 1425-1449. https://doi.org/10.1007/s11423-017-9520-7

Swain, M. (1995). Three functions of output in second language learning. In G. Cook & B. Seidlhofer (Eds.), *Principles and practice in the study of language* (pp. 125–144). Oxford University Press.

Tomlinson, B., & Masuhara, H. (2018). *The complete guide to the theory and practice of materials development for language learning.* John Wiley & Sons.

Williams, J., & Evans, J. (1998). What kind of focus and on what forms? In C. Doughty & J. Williams (Eds.), *Focus on form in classroom second language acquisition* (pp. 139–155). Cambridge University Press.

(Campbell, 2023, pp. 10–13)

The following example activity (Çıraklı & Kılıçkaya, 2023) describes how a digital collaboration activity based on collaborative writing can be implemented with an AI tool.

Activity Title	Integrating artificial intelligence into collaborative poetry
Introduction	This activity integrates artificial intelligence (AI) into students' collaborative writing. The activity allows students to create their poems working in groups via the use of AI.
Target Language	English
Target Language Skills & Areas	Writing and speaking
Learner Levels	High school/university students (B1/B2 in the Common European Framework of Reference for Languages (CEFR))
Activity Aims	This activity aims to allow students to work together to create a poem by benefiting *ChatGPT* and improve their collaborative and critical thinking skills while working on tasks.
Activity Length	40 minutes
Preparation Time	20 minutes
Technical Requirements & Resources	Internet-connected computers/laptops for students; A projector; *OpenAI* (https://openai.com/); *Padlet* (https://www.padlet.com/); *Canva* (https://www.canva.com/); *Rhymer* (https://www.rhymer.com/)
Procedure	1. Students are given a stanza from William Blake's "Songs of Innocence" and asked to imagine someone with the feelings of loss aroused by the following lines: *When my mother died I was very young, And my father sold me while yet my tongue Could scarcely cry' 'weep! 'weep! 'weep! 'weep!' So your chimneys I sweep & in soot I sleep.* 2. The students are then asked to work in groups of four or five depending on the class size and write together another stanza that could follow the given stanza. Each student can be assigned a different role in the poem. For example, one person could be responsible for coming up with the opening line, another could write the middle section, and someone else could write the ending. Alternatively, the students can take turns adding lines to the poem. Once everyone has had a chance to add a line or two, they can read the poem aloud to see how it sounds.

Continued....

	3. When the students are finished with their writing, they are asked to visit the website *OpenAI* (https://openai.com/) and write the following instruction in the playground: "Please continue the following stanza."
4. The students are asked to compare and contrast their stanza with the one created by *ChatGPT* and revise their stanza to finalize it.
5. Then, the students are asked to share their stanza on *Padlet* (https://www.padlet.com/) and vote for the stanza that would best follow the very first stanza provided at the beginning of the class. They are also encouraged to express their comments and suggestions on the works of other groups.
Options and Suggestions	• As a project, working in pairs or in groups, students can create a poster for their poems on *Canva* (https://www.canva.com/).
• Students can be given poems written by the AI language model in Step 3. However, the last word in each line can be removed and students can be asked to find a suitable word for these blanks. For this purpose, they can use *Rhymer* (https://www.rhymer.com/).
Justification	This activity allows students to use their creativity and to think about words, language, and feelings in new ways (Grainger et al., 2005). Students are given a stanza of a poem as a prompt to write the second stanza and also asked to benefit from AI language models to compare and contrast different versions. This notion of discordance is a crucial point in creation, more than accordance. Creativity comes interestingly out of distortion, and students are keenly drawn to the discrepancies, differences, disillusionment, and disintegration between the AI product and human versions. The variety of the use of language and verbal arrangements will make students be amazed by the flexibility of the patterns, feasibility of the verbal storage, and fancy of the user imagination (Çıraklı, 2018). Thus, collaborative poetry can be a great way to connect with others (Storch, 2011) and to express their creativity (Golden, 2000). Moreover, the AI product can provide students with a peculiar mirror by which they can reflect upon their own

Continued....

creative practice and cognitive praxis (Southgate, 2021). Working with others, students may not merely draw on or bring their own perspectives to the writing bench but also can distort and test their writings according to the AI product. This act of mirroring and contrasting is a bilateral process through which students raise critical, cognitive, and creative questions as to how the different versions vary, including verbal, semantic, semiotic, syntagmatic, and stylistic variations and deviations (Çıraklı, 2022).

References and Further Reading

Adams, R. (2022). Second language writing and technology. In N. Ziegler & M. González-Lloret (Eds.), *Routledge handbook of second language acquisition and technology* (pp. 187–200). Routledge. https://doi.org/10.4324/9781351117586-17

Çıraklı, M. Z. (2018). Theory of postromantic education in the postmodernist era: Maxims. *Journal of Narrative and Language Studies*, *6*(11), 133-136. http://nalans.com/index.php/nalans/article/view/127

Çıraklı, M. Z. (2022). Loss of spatial interaction in virtual environments and the improvement of cognition: Online literature classroom through Adobe Connect. In F. Kılıçkaya, J. Kic-Drgas, & R. Nahlen (Eds.), *The challenges and opportunities of teaching English worldwide in the COVID-19 pandemic* (pp. 183–191). Cambridge Scholars Publishing.

Godwin-Jones, R. (2021). Evolving technologies for language learning. *Language Learning & Technology, 25*(3), 6-26. https://doi.org/10125/73443

Golden, K. (2000). The use of collaborative writing to enhance cohesion in poetry therapy groups. *Journal of Poetry Therapy, 13*, 125-138. https://doi.org/10.1023/A:1021473712505

Grainger, T., Goouch, K., & Lambirth, A. (2005). *Creativity and writing: Developing voice and verse in the classroom*. Routledge. https://doi.org/10.4324/9780203391075

Lai, C. (2017). *Autonomous language learning with technology: Beyond the classroom*. Bloomsbury.

Son, J.-B. (2017). *Online activities for language learning*. http://drjbson.com/projects/oall/

Son, J.-B. (2011). Online tools for language teaching. *TESL-EJ, 15*(1). https://tesl-ej.org/wordpress/issues/volume15/ej57/ej57int/

Continued....

Southgate, E. (2021). Artificial intelligence and machine learning: A practical and ethical guide for teachers. In C. Wyatt-Smith, B. Lingard, & E. Heck (Eds.), *Digital disruption in teaching and testing: Assessments, big data, and the transformation of schooling* (pp. 60–74). Routledge. https://doi.org/10.4324/9781003045793

Storch, N. (2011). Collaborative writing in L2 contexts: Processes, outcomes, and future directions. *Annual Review of Applied Linguistics, 31*, 275-288. https://doi.org/10.1017/S0267190511000079

(Çıraklı & Kılıçkaya, 2023, pp. 70–73)

Task 5.2

Evaluate each activity given in Section 5.2 by asking the following questions:
- How collaborate is the activity?
- Is the activity suitable for students in your context?
- Does the activity have appropriate scope for the use of collaboration strategies?

Discussion Questions

1. What is effective collaboration?
2. What do you think about group work in online environments?
3. What tools do you use to collaborate with others online?
4. What social rules do students need to know in digital collaboration?
5. What strategies do you use to teach digital collaboration in your context?
6. How can teachers teach students intercultural collaboration in digital spaces?
7. What is the role of collaboration in digital language teacher development?
8. What skills and strategies do language teachers and students need to develop for effective digital collaboration?
9. How can teachers help students use digital technologies effectively for collaborative language learning?
10. How can teachers provide students with authentic opportunities to develop digital collaboration skills in the classroom and out of the classroom?

6
Online Safety

The safe use of technology is crucial in the digital world. While the widespread use of digital technologies offers new opportunities for information search, creation, communication, and collaboration, it raises online safety (also known as internet safety, cybersafety, or e-safety) issues such as cyberbullying, invasion of privacy, identity theft, and exposure to harmful content. Thus, there is a great need for us to address those issues in online spaces. As we spend more time on the internet, we face more risks to monitor and manage. In the field of language education, it is important for language learners and teachers to develop their online safety skills to stay safe and strengthen their safety practices more than ever. This chapter discusses the meaning of being safe online and how to develop online safety skills in language learning and teaching.

6.1 Being safe online

There are safety issues in the use of digital technologies and services. Our concerns about online safety are growing along with the increase of online scams, malicious software (malware) threats, and identity theft in digital environments. We need to be vigilant in addressing the concerns and make sure that our devices, information, and privacy are as secure as possible. Otherwise, we might face the risks of online victimisation. Thus, online safety skills are indispensable in our digital lives.

Online safety is the act of being aware of safety and security risks and protecting ourselves from the risks online. Its importance has been highlighted in many publications (e.g., Buckingham, 2015; eSafety Commissioner, 2021; Katz, 2012). Language learners and teachers need to be trained to protect and manage their personal data and avoid harmful experiences online. They need to be cautious about the information that is shared online and take steps to protect sensitive information. They also need to be cautious about clicking on suspicious links or downloading files from unknown sources and be responsible and ethical in the use of online materials.

There are public and policy concerns over e-safety (Hague & Payton, 2010). Payton and Hague (2010) explained that e-safety is relevant to "the development of safe practices when using digital technologies such as the internet and mobile phones" and it includes "developing understandings of what constitutes appropriate use of digital technologies and the development of a critical reflection about the sort of content that is being made public" (p. 62). Hague and Payton (2010) said, "When seeking to develop students' digital literacy", it is important that "teachers make explicit links to e-safety – whether this be about age appropriate content, concern over the predatory behaviour of adults, acceptable use and cyber-bullying or issues of plagiarism, copyright and virus protection" (p. 44).

Shillair et al. (2015) pointed out that many internet users still do not follow online safety standards despite online security concerns. In a survey study on the interplay among user knowledge, personal responsibility, and training techniques, they suggested that intervention strategies should match the knowledge level of the user to enhance online safety behaviours. In another study on online safety behaviours, Dodel and Mesch (2018) found that digital security skills and antivirus behaviours are unequally distributed among Israeli internet users and have strong associations with social dimensions of inequality such as gender, age, and education. To increase online safety awareness effectively, Mohammad et al. (2022) argued that human factors such as biological, psychological, and cultural factors should be considered holistically.

Walsh et al. (2022) described the development of a framework for online safety education and presented the following five key elements of the framework:

1. Students' rights and responsibilities. Online safety education should be based on recognising, acknowledging, and understanding students' rights and responsibilities in the digital age.
2. Resilience and risk. Online safety education positively frames the use of technology, while also building awareness of factors that decrease and increase risk of harm.
3. Effective whole-school approaches. Online safety education is underpinned by effective whole-school approaches for promoting student wellbeing and preventing student harm.
4. Integrated and specific curriculum. Online safety education builds knowledge and skills across the curriculum. It includes both technical and relational (interpersonal) aspects needed to navigate digital environments and develops student agency to use what they have learned in practice.

5. Continuous improvement through review and evaluation. Online safety education is continuously improved using the best available evidence, data and authoritative information from eSafety about online safety issues, risks and harms. (p. 9)

Based on the analysis of data collected from a series of workshops with seven classes of 10 to 12-year-old students in three primary schools in Finland, Hartikainen et al. (2019) made the following design recommendations for online safety education:

1. Integrate aspects of children's own media culture = respect their wish in relation to Tradition and increase Hedonism. It is important to note that children were easily distracted and annoyed when video design, game design, or user interface and control design were not top quality or did not conform to standards, thus decreasing Hedonistic value of the educational package, and Stimulation it provides.
2. Have a positive tone, as there are also valuable things online = respect their wish in relation to Tradition, increase Stimulation.
3. Include more concrete advice instead of vague warnings = increase Self-direction, Security.
4. Engage the children in the design and evaluation = increase Self-direction.
5. Engage also the teacher = an engaged teacher increases pupil's Stimulation. (p.14)

Shin (2015) highlighted the need for online safety education and said, "When planning lessons, teachers need to be mindful not to put students at risk, and should teach children concrete strategies to protect themselves" (p. 185). In his study on the effects of the design and analysis of language lessons using online materials on pre-service EFL teachers' awareness of digital literacy, fair use of digital materials, and e-safety, he found that, when planning the lessons, the pre-service teachers initially did not give serious consideration to copyright and e-safety-related issues; however, after evaluation activities, they showed an increase in their awareness of the critical, ethical, and safe use of online materials. He suggested that the responsible and safe use of technology should be modelled in teacher education programs. In a different context, Vartiainen et al. (2022) conducted and analysed interviews with 14 Finnish pre-service teachers about their conceptions and experiences of data agency in social media environments. They found that the pre-service teachers constructed their data agency in terms of social norms and recognised their lack of understanding of wider socio-technical systems within which data agencies are situated. They argued that pre-service teachers need to have "a sophisticated understanding of commercial-level issues and related mechanisms of ML (machine learning) and data-driven approaches to automation" (p. 15) to teach children and youth in a data-driven society.

Ferrari's (2013) digital competence in safety include: protecting devices; protecting personal data; protecting health; and protecting the environment. In her self-assessment grid, the advanced level of safety is described as follows:

> I frequently update my security strategies. I can take action when the device is under threat. I often change the default privacy settings of online services to enhance my privacy protection. I have an informed and wide understanding of privacy issues and I know how my data is collected and used. I am aware of the correct use of technologies to avoid health problems. I know how to find a good balance between online and off-line worlds. I have an informed stance on the impact of technologies on everyday life, online consumption, and the environment. (p. 14)

The Australian Curriculum, Assessment and Reporting Authority (ACARA) (2021), on the other hand, described three sub-elements of practising digital safety and wellbeing as follows:

- Manage digital wellbeing – Students understand the nature and impact of technology use on their health, work productivity, wellbeing and lifestyles, such as excessive screen time and multi-tasking.
- Manage online privacy and safety – Students develop the appropriate technical, social, cognitive, communicative and decision-making skills to address online risks. They recognise the content risks that they face online, such as hurtful user-generated content, and the strategies involved in dealing with them.
- Manage digital identity – Students recognise the importance of controlling and shaping their own digital identity by creating and curating their online identities to positively tell their stories, while recognising how personal use of digital media may have implications. (pp. 7–8)

The TESOL Technology Standards Framework (TESOL, 2008) also has specific statements relevant to the safe use of technology in its technology standards for language learners and language teachers. In Goal 1, Standard 3 of technology standards for language learners ("Language learners exercise appropriate caution when using online sources and when engaging in electronic communication" (p. 23)), it stated the following performance indicators:

- Language learners are cautious when opening attachments and clicking on links in email messages.
- Language learners have security software running on their own computers and other devices and keep them current (e.g., antivirus and firewall software).
- Underage students do not provide personal contact information except as directed by the teacher; adult students exercise caution.
- Language learners exercise caution in computer-mediated communication (CMC) (e.g., log out/off when leaving an email account or a public computer; protect personal information).
- Language learners demonstrate their understanding of the fact that placing any information or content online can become part of a permanent record.
- Language learners identify examples of false and potentially malicious information that exists online. (p. 23)

In Goal 1, Standard 4 of technology standards for language teachers ("Language teachers use technology in socially and culturally appropriate, legal, and ethical ways" (p. 31)), it stated the following performance indicators:

- Language teachers demonstrate sensitivity to the similarities and differences in communication conventions across cultures, communities, and contexts.
- Language teachers show an awareness of their role as models, demonstrating respect for others in their use of public and private information.
- Language teachers show awareness and understanding when approaching culturally sensitive topics and offer students alternatives.
- Language teachers conform to local legal requirements regarding the privacy of students' personal information.
- Language teachers conform to local legal requirements regarding accessibility.
- Language teachers conform to local legal requirements regarding fair use and copyright.

- Language teachers follow local guidelines regarding the use of human subjects for research.
- Language teachers demonstrate awareness that electronic communication is not secure and private, and that in some localities, email may be subject to "open records" laws.
- Language teachers seek help in identifying and implementing solutions related to legal requirements.
- Language teachers protect student privacy (e.g., not inappropriately putting student email addresses, biodata, or photos online; fully informing students about public sharing of blogs and web sites; using password-protected sites when possible).
- Language teachers respect student ownership of their own work (e.g., not sharing student work inappropriately; not requiring students to post their work publicly). (pp. 31–32)

These indicators provide useful information and additional measures for language learners and language teachers who work in online environments. Hubbard (2021) reminded us that "security and safety are issues at any time online for both students and teachers" (p. 14) and teachers need to "protect student safety and privacy when asking them to publish any of their work online" (p. 36). He proposed the following questions for further discussion: "What do you know about the differences between the static (at home or in the classroom) and mobile environments you and your students work in? How reliable are they? How secure are they? How private are they? How equitable are they? In exploring these questions, take notes to help you understand and possibly improve your settings" (p. 23). It should be a good practice for language teachers and learners to keep asking online safety-related questions themselves in and out of the classroom.

Task 6.1

Explore ways of protecting devices and personal data online and discuss what digital safety activities can be used in the language classroom.

6.2 Developing online safety skills

Developing online safety skills is a critical component of digital literacy training. There are many resources that support online safety education.

For example, classroom resources of Australia's eSafety Commissioner (https://www.esafety.gov.au/educators/classroom-resources) and resources from the Student Wellbeing Hub (https://studentwellbeinghub.edu.au/educators/topics/online-safety/). Language learners need skills to stay safe while exploring and using online language learning materials available on the internet. To help language learners develop the skills, language teachers need to employ effective strategies (e.g., promoting online safety through example cases, modelling online behaviour). They can also teach online safety skills through online safety activities in language lessons and integrate them into their language learning curriculum.

As part of remote teaching tips offered through the British Council, Donaghy (n.d.) shares the following online safety lesson ideas, which guide teachers to keep their learners safe in an online context:

- Online lesson agreement: Work with the learners to write a classroom charter or set of rules. This is an excellent way for learners and teachers to collaborate and agree on expected behaviours, interactions, dress codes and consequences. You can draw attention to this in the introduction to each session.
- What to do if we're unhappy: Ask learners what sorts of things may make them unhappy and when they may need to tell a teacher or adult. For example, 'if someone contacts you out of the class', 'if someone posts a photo of you online' or 'if someone says something nasty to you'. Show learners how they can report a concern on your online learning system or via teacher chat.
- Expect respect: Share a story about someone who has had hurtful things written online. Stop and ask your learners how they think the story will end. Share the ending and discuss. What should you do if you see hurtful online posts about someone in your class? Demonstrate that you respect your learners and remind them to respect each other, as in the normal classroom. If you detect bullying, report it through established channels.
- Cyber quizmasters: Ask learners to write a quiz on e-safety for them to ask their family members. For example: To ensure my password is secure it should (a) use three random words; (b) not include personal information such as a child or pet name; and (c) be a different password for every service. (p. 2)

Wishart et al. (2007) investigated the use of an online role play activity aimed to teach 9 to 12-year-old school children about internet safety and suggested that technical issues and issues with learners' comprehension and expectations of the task must be resolved before online interaction can generate learning. They emphasised the importance of preparation as noted in the following recommendations: "Preparation of teachers can be improved by providing step by step instructions about how the activity runs, to include screen shots or a simulation"; "Clear directions should be provided for teachers about how to induct their pupils into the activity to include preparation for role, guidance on types of questions to ask and on expected number and frequency of replies" (p. 472).

From a broad perspective, Ribble (n.d.) considered digital citizenship as "the continuously developing norms of appropriate, responsible, and empowered technology use" and presented the following nine elements:

1. Digital access: the equitable distribution of technology and online resources.
2. Digital commerce: the electronic buying and selling of goods and focuses on the tools and safeguards in place to assist those buying, selling, banking, or using money in any way in the digital space.
3. Digital communication and collaboration: the electronic exchange of information.
4. Digital etiquette: electronic standards of conduct or procedures and has to do with the process of thinking about others when using digital devices.
5. Digital fluency: the process of understanding technology and its use.
6. Digital health and welfare: the physical and psychological well-being in a digital world.
7. Digital law: the electronic responsibility for actions and deeds and has to do with the creation of rules and policy that address issues related to the online world.
8. Digital rights and responsibility: those requirements and freedoms extended to everyone in a digital world.
9. Digital security and privacy: the electronic precautions to guarantee safety.

The International Society for Technology in Education (ISTE) has the ISTE Standards for Educators (https://iste.org/standards/educators) describing educators' seven roles: learner; leader, citizen; collaborator; designer; facilitator; and analyst. The citizen role, in particular, is closely related to digital data management and guides educators to do the following:

3. Citizen

Educators inspire students to positively contribute to and responsibly participate in the digital world. Educators:

a. Create experiences for learners to make positive, socially responsible contributions and exhibit empathetic behavior online that build relationships and community.
b. Establish a learning culture that promotes curiosity and critical examination of online resources and fosters digital literacy and media fluency.
c. Mentor students in safe, legal and ethical practices with digital tools and the protection of intellectual rights and property.
d. Model and promote management of personal data and digital identity and protect student data privacy.

Gleason and von Gillern (2018) pointed out a need for digital citizenship curricula to stress "the real-life experience, values, and personal interests and engagement of young people themselves" (p. 200). They suggested that the use of social media (e.g., *Twitter*) in formal and informal learning spaces can support the development of digital citizenship for secondary school students. They recommended that teachers who are responsible for teaching digital citizenship should consider integrating social media as a way to develop learning networks. In Hong Kong, Gu et al. (2023) examined how a group of university students understand digital citizenship and construct it through digital literacy practices. They found that all their participants perceived digital citizenship as the possession of online skills and participation in social and cultural activities in online spaces. They also found that the participants synergised different languages and semiotic systems for meaning making in communication in social media. They recommended educators and educational institutions to consider "establishing/enhancing digital literacy education curriculum with the following purposes: a) enhancing value education of empathy, morality and ethical behavior in virtual contexts; b) developing or enhancing diverse digital communicative competences for activities with a wide range of goals such as career development, formal and informal learning, social networking, well-being, maintenance in complex social and cultural contexts" (p. 10). The digital literacy curriculum would need to compass the knowledge, skills, and attitudes that students need for their participation in digital social networks.

Example activities for developing online safety skills in the language classroom are given below.

Activity 6.1

Digital footprint and privacy

Introduction	This activity is designed to introduce the idea of a digital footprint to students and reflect on their own online presence and activities. It encourages students to track and manage the information they leave behind when they use the internet.
Target Language	English
Target Language Skills & Areas	Reading, writing, listening, and speaking
Learner Levels	Intermediate to advanced levels
Activity Length	30–50 minutes
Preparation Time	30–50 minutes
Technical Requirements & Resources	A computer for each student or each group *YouTube* (https://www.youtube.com/) A virtual wall such as *Padlet* (https://padlet.com/) or *Netboard.me* (https://netboard.me/) Web search engines such as *Google* (https://www.google.com/) and *Bing* (https://www.bing.com/)
Procedure	1. Assign students a task (e.g., summarising the content of a video about online privacy, reviewing privacy settings, deleting old posts or online accounts, creating a plan for managing their digital footprint). 2. Guide the students to visit the Teaching Privacy website (https://teachingprivacy.org/) and explore the relevant contents of the website and/or watch a video, which is related to their task, from the Teaching Privacy YouTube channel (https://www.youtube.com/channel/UCxJyunaDKG_iqmS5C1RgocQ). 3. Encourage the students to summarise what they read and/or watch and make a list of questions to explore further.

Continued....

Activity 6.1 *Continued....*

	4. Ask the students to post their written reports to a virtual wall. 5. Invite the students to discuss the posts shown on the virtual wall. 6. Give feedback on the posts and discussions.
Options and Suggestions	• The teacher can prepare relevant questions students can explore and answer through the activity. • The teacher can guide students to discuss practical ways of making their digital footprint smaller.

Activity 6.2

Online safety quiz

Introduction	This activity utilises online quizzes to test students' knowledge about online safety. It enhances students' understanding of online safety and encourages their knowledge building.
Target Language	Any language
Target Language Skills & Areas	Reading and writing
Learner Levels	All levels
Activity Length	30–50 minutes
Preparation Time	30–50 minutes
Technical Requirements & Resources	A computer for each student or each group An online quiz creation tool such as *Kahoot!* (https://kahoot.com/) or *Quizlet* (https://quizlet.com/)
Procedure	1. Choose topics to cover in the quiz (e.g., protecting personal information, using secure passwords, avoiding scams). 2. Make quiz questions by using an online quiz creation tool. Alternatively, the following example quizzes (English) can be considered: eSafety Commissioner's Be Secure Quiz (https://www.esafety.gov.au/educators/classroom-resources/be-secure/quiz); GCF Global's Internet Safety Quiz (https://edu.gcfglobal.org/en/internetsafety/internet-safety-quiz/1/)

Continued....

Activity 6.2 *Continued....*

	3. Decide how the activity will be implemented (e.g., individual tests, small group work, the whole class activity). 4. Ask students to take the quiz online in the suggested format. 5. Guide the students to use their knowledge and experience in answering the quiz questions. 6. Give feedback on the results of the quiz. 7. Discuss what the students have learned from the activity.
Options and Suggestions	• The teacher can consider a variety of topics students need to know. • The teacher can collate and present which particular questions need more exploration and explanation.

Activity 6.3

Online safety video

Introduction	This activity gives students opportunities to reflect on their online safety practices. It enhances online safety awareness and knowledge.
Target Language	English
Target Language Skills & Areas	Listening and speaking
Learner Levels	All levels
Activity Length	30–50 minutes
Preparation Time	30–50 minutes
Technical Requirements & Resources	A computer for each student or each group A video sharing tool such as *SchoolTube* (https://schooltube.com/), *WatchKnowLearn.org* (http://www.watchknowlearn.org/), or *YouTube* (https://www.youtube.com/) An online whiteboard such as *Zoom Whiteboard* (https://explore.zoom.us/en/products/online-whiteboard/), *Microsoft Whiteboard* (https://www.microsoft.com/en-au/microsoft-365/microsoft-whiteboard/), *Miro* (https://miro.com/), or *Mural* (https://mural.co/)

Continued....

Activity 6.3 *Continued....*

Procedure	1. Guide students to watch a video about cyberbullying, using social media responsibly, or other topics related to online safety. Example videos can be found from eSafety Commissioner's video library for educators (https://www.esafety.gov.au/educators/video-library).
2. Ask the students to reflect on their online safety practices while watching the video.
3. Invite the students to discuss what they have learned from the video.
4. Encourage the students to make suggestions for good ways of protecting themselves and others online.
5. Make a summary of the suggestions.
Options and Suggestions	• The teacher can come out with a variety of topics, issues, and questions that students can discuss online.
• The teacher can consider using an online whiteboard when students have group discussions.

Activity 6.4

Being a digital citizen

Introduction	This activity is designed to teach students about digital citizenship. It guides students to engage in online communities safely and responsibly.
Target Language	English
Target Language Skills & Areas	Reading, writing, listening, and speaking
Learner Levels	Intermediate to advanced levels
Activity Length	30–50 minutes
Preparation Time	30–50 minutes
Technical Requirements & Resources	A computer for each student or each group
A virtual wall such as *Padlet* (https://padlet.com/) or *Netboard.me* (https://netboard.me/)
Web search engines such as *Google* (https://www.google.com/) and *Bing* (https://www.bing.com/)

Continued....

Activity 6.4 *Continued....*

Procedure	1. Make and implement a digital citizenship lesson. Alternatively, the following lessons and resources can be used or adapted: Common Sense Education's digital citizenship lessons (https://www.commonsense.org/education/digital-citizenship); PBS Learning Media's digital citizenship resources (https://www.pbslearningmedia.org/subjects/engineering--technology/technological-literacy/digital-citizenship/)
2. Give students instructions on how to participate in the activity and what they need to do.
3. Guide the students to share their ideas on a virtual wall.
4. Encourage the students to consider various ways of being a good digital citizen.
5. Invite the students to discuss the posts made on the virtual wall.
6. Give guidance and feedback whenever needed.
7. Have a group discussion about what the students learnt from the activity.
Options and Suggestions	• The teacher can consider using various topics, themes, or questions to explore.
• The teacher can make clear connections with students' digital lifestyles.

Additional Activities

In an evaluation of an online role play activity called Net-Detectives, Wishart et al. (2007) reported that the pupils in their study enjoyed being detectives. One of eSafety Commissioner's classroom resources (https://www.esafety.gov.au/educators/classroom-resources/cybersmart-challenge) also uses the idea of letting pupils play the role of detectives. It is called Cybersmart Detectives. The following is a brief description of the activity, which deals with issues of inappropriate or unwanted contact, privacy and personal information, respectful online behaviour, and accessing support.

Key outcomes

By the end of this unit of work, students will be able to:

- identify what personal information is safe to put online;
- describe and use strategies in situations where they feel uncomfortable or unsafe online;
- recognise that people they meet online may pretend to be someone else; and
- seek assistance if things go wrong online.

Activity

- Part 1 (20–25 mins): Show the students the animation (https://www.esafety.gov.au/educators/classroom-resources/cybersmart-challenge/cybersmart-detectives) and lead a discussion based on suggested questions provided.
- Part 2 (30 mins, immediately after Part 1 or as a separate lesson): Students create a personal profile suitable to be posted online. Students create a list of trusted people they would contact if an online experience made them uncomfortable.

The following example activity from eSafety Commissioner is called Cybersmart Hero, which deals with issues of cyberbullying, bystanders, respectful online behaviour, and accessing support.

Key outcomes

By the end of this unit of work, students will be able to:

- identify what cyberbullying is;
- describe and use strategies in situations where they feel cyberbullied;
- recognise when to seek help in cyberbullying situations; and
- be a positive bystander in a cyberbullying situation.

Activity

- Part 1 (20–25 mins): Show the students the animation (https://www.esafety.gov.au/educators/classroom-resources/cybersmart-challenge/cybersmart-hero) and lead a discussion based on suggested questions provided.

- Part 2 (30 mins, immediately after Part 1 or as a separate lesson): Students identify and discuss whether a range of scenarios are examples of cyberbullying, bullying, or not bullying.

Task 6.2

Evaluate each activity given in Section 6.2 by asking the following questions:

- Is the activity suitable for students in your context?
- Does the activity have appropriate scope for the use of online safety strategies?
- How can the activity be integrated into language lessons?

Discussion Questions

1. How do you identify whether a specific website is safe to be used for your teaching?
2. How do you measure the size of your digital footprint?
3. What actions do you take to make your digital footprint smaller?
4. How do your privacy settings affect your online safety?
5. What is the role of online safety in digital language learning and teaching?
6. What sort of critical questioning might you need to support students' online safety?
7. How do you know when you need to intervene for online safety of language learners?
8. What skills and strategies do language teachers and students need to develop for online safety?
9. How can teachers help students use online materials critically, ethically, and safely?
10. How can teachers provide students with authentic opportunities to develop online safety skills in the classroom and out of the classroom?

7
Digital Language Teaching

Digital language teaching refers to "the application of digital pedagogies and technologies to the teaching of languages" (Son, 2020b, p. 3). It involves the use of digital tools and resources that support language learning and teaching. Figure 7.1 shows main bases of digital language teaching: digital literacy, digital pedagogies, and digital technologies. Digital language teaching requires digital literacy as a basic requirement and is implemented with digital pedagogies and digital technologies. The target language to teach is considered throughout all lines that connect each element. For the success of digital language teaching, it is essential for language teachers to have competent digital literacy skills, use digital teaching strategies, and integrate technologies effectively into language teaching. Language teachers need to provide language learners with interactive, dynamic, and engaging learning experiences and appropriate guidance and feedback in digital environments. This chapter explores the connection between digital literacy education and language teaching with digital pedagogies and digital technologies and discusses how language teachers can develop digital language teaching skills.

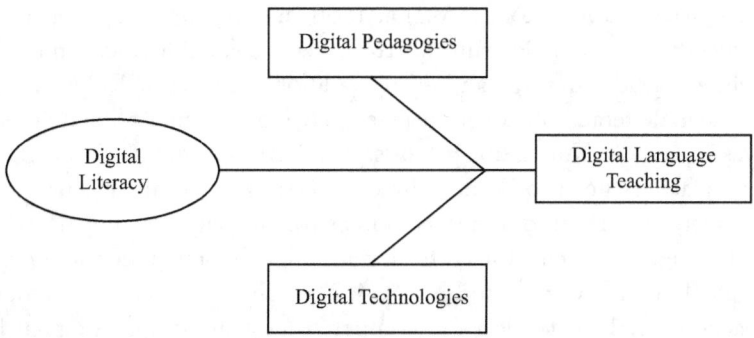

Figure 7.1 *Bases of Digital Language Teaching*

7.1 Digital literacy education and language teaching

Digital literacy has received great attention in research on language learning and teaching (Davin & Hafner, 2022; Godwin-Jones, 2016). For example, there have been many studies that investigated L2/FL learners' digital literacy levels (e.g., Dashtestani & Hojatpanah, 2022; Kang & Kim, 2021; Nguyen & Habók, 2022; Seghayer, 2020; Son et al., 2017), which were similar to or different from studies of the levels of students' digital literacy or competence in the field of education (e.g., Fraga-Varela & Alonso-Ferreiro, 2022; Gui & Argentin, 2011; Karagul et al., 2021; Porat et al., 2018). There were also studies of digital literacy levels and/or practices of pre-service language teachers (e.g., Akayoğlu et al., 2020) and in-service language teachers (e.g., Cote & Milliner, 2018; Dashtestani & Hojatpanah, 2021).

Son et al. (2017), specifically, presented the results of two studies of the digital literacy levels of two different groups of English language learners in Australia and Japan. They found that all participants in the two studies were interested in using digital technologies while each group showed a different level of expectations and needs in their digital literacy skills. They also found that there was a difference between self-competency and actual knowledge of digital literacy, which was a similar finding of Son et al. (2011), and pointed out that learners' self-assessment of digital literacy skills does not always reflect their practical knowledge of digital literacy. Another finding was that the lack of knowledge of learners was selected by both groups as the most common factor affecting the use of digital technologies for language learning. It implies the need for learner training (Hubbard, 2013; Son, 2019).

As mentioned by Godwin-Jones (2015), digital literacy is often stated as a common goal of many language programs these days. It is directly related to the ability to use digital tools and resources appropriately for specific purposes. Pegrum (2016) noted, "Digital literacies must be taught alongside language and more traditional literacy skills" (p. 9). To teach digital literacy, obviously, teachers have to be digitally literate themselves (Hauck & Kurek, 2017; Korisztek, 2021; Yuan et al., 2019). Language teachers need to be digitally competent to critically evaluate and effectively use digital tools and resources for language teaching. In other words, language teachers need to develop digital competence supported by digital literacy. Carrier and Nye (2017) made the following comment: "Teachers need to develop the competencies that comprise digital literacy in order to take advantage of what technology enhancement and enabling can provide" (p. 220).

Ally (2019) proposed a competency profile for digital teachers who must be able to educate students in online environments using emerging digital technologies. The profile included the following competencies required by digital teachers for future education: general qualities; using digital technology; developing digital learning resources; re-mixing learning resources; communicating with learners; facilitating learning; pedagogical strategies; assessing learning; and personal characteristics. Through a systematic review on digital literacy, on the other hand, Tinmaz et al. (2022) identified four major themes revealed from their qualitative content analysis of 43 reviewed articles: digital literacy, digital competencies, digital skills, and digital thinking. They reported that, among the four themes, digital competencies were related to problem solving, safety, information processing, content creation, and communication.

Calling for cooperation in digital education, European Commission (2020) released their Digital Education Action Plan 2021–2027 to foster the development of a high-performing digital education ecosystem and enhance digital skills and competences for the digital transformation on the national, European, and international level. In emergency remote teaching in Hong Kong, locally, Wong and Moorhouse (2021) examined primary and secondary school English language teachers' digital competence and found that "adaptability was a critical theme for teacher digital competence with language instruction and assessments" (p. 10).

Language teachers can teach language learners to combine their linguistic skills and digital skills and to be digitally literate in the digitally connected world while considering needs of language learners in the digital age. However, Guikema and Menke (2014) argued that teacher preparation programs "are not adequately raising FL teacher candidates' awareness of the need to address digital literacies, and, consequently, teacher candidates are not prepared to integrate digital literacies into instruction" (p. 280). They suggested a reconceptualisation of language teacher education based on an expanded view of literacy, including digital literacy, in foreign language instruction. Many teachers find curricular integration difficult when they encourage students to do out-of-class online activities (Godwin-Jones, 2015). In a study of the evaluation of technology integration in a Vietnamese university language program, Gruba and Nguyen (2019) found that students' low digital literacy was a challenge together with lecturers' professional development. In another study with in-service teachers who were enrolled in a master's degree at an American university, Zoch et al. (2017) reported that the teachers found testing a challenging barrier to technology integration.

Carrier and Nye (2017) asked the question of what digital teachers need to know to be digitally literate in a manner that enhances their teaching and supports their students' learning. They suggested that digital teachers need to know about new pedagogical models and new digital learning channels. Meniado (2023) emphasised that both pre-service and in-service teachers need to be prepared for the digital future and recommended:

> They must be skilled in designing equitable, diversified and inclusive learning opportunities that serve the unique learning needs and purposes of learners. They must also be skilled in evaluating and utilizing varied forms of technologies that can facilitate various modes of instructional delivery, assessment and giving feedback. Lastly, they must be skilled in using technologies that allow them to develop themselves professionally and collaborate with fellow professionals in order to solve learning problems and innovate learning solutions. (p. 470)

Digital literacy education is clearly required for online learning and teaching as mentioned by Karagul et al. (2021) who discussed educational challenges brought out by the COVID-19 pandemic and said, "The abrupt transition from face-to-face to online education has created the need for some specific abilities, such as digital literacy on the side of the learners at all educational levels" (p. 1). Jones (2021) suggested that digital literacy education should "engage students in critically evaluating how technologies work" through "getting them to reflect on their subjective experiences of 'working with' and being 'worked on by' technologies" (p. 7). More broadly, Bacalja et al. (2022) raised the question of what digital literacy education constitutes and suggested that digital literacy education should include a focus on critical digital literacies. They said, "The rise of digital literacies associated with datafication, AI, platformatisation, algorhythmic learning, and big data, to name a few, raises further questions about the very nature of digital literacy in schools, what should constitute a digital literacy education, and what role teachers should have in preparing young people for a future digital citizenship" (p. 257). They also stated, "Building knowledge in this field, and providing preservice and practising teachers with information, strategies and resources is patently a clear task for literacy educators, as for the profession as a whole" (p. 261).

Hafner (2014) described a university course in English for science, which incorporated digital literacy practices in the form of a digital video project, and suggested a pedagogical approach that "embeds digital literacy practices alongside more traditional literacy practices" (p. 656). The combination of traditional literacy practices and digital literacy practices could be a teaching idea for teachers to consider. In a qualitative study on the relationship between language teachers' personal and professional use of digital technologies, Tour (2015) highlighted the power of digital mindsets and reported that her three participants' digital literacy practices were shaped by their digital mindsets, which comprised assumptions about affordances of digital technologies. From a different angle, Darvin and Hafner (2022) emphasised the importance of understanding what teaching digital literacies today means and the need for further research on how to design and implement digital literacy instruction.

In their position statement on 21st century literacies, the National Council of Teachers of English (2007) underlined an integrated approach to literacy instruction and included the following recommendations for teachers:

- Encourage students to reflect regularly about the role of technology in their learning.
- Create a website and invite students to use it to continue class discussions and bring in outside voices.
- Give students strategies for evaluating the quality of information they find on the internet.
- Be open about your own strengths and limitations with technology and invite students to help you.
- Explore technologies students are using outside of class and find ways to incorporate them into your teaching.
- Use a wiki to develop a multimodal reader's guide to a class text.
- Include a broad variety of media and genres in class texts.
- Ask students to create a podcast to share with an authentic audience.
- Give students explicit instruction about how to avoid plagiarism in a digital environment. (p. 18)

These suggestions can be adapted and applied to classroom instruction or self-directed study through practical learning and teaching activities.

Task 7.1a

What kinds of activities would you expect to explore and experience in a workshop on digital literacy education? Explain your answer.

Task 7.1b

Son (2015) developed two digital literacy questionnaires: Digital Literacy Questionnaire – Language Learners (DLQ-LL) and Digital Literacy Questionnaire – Language Teachers (DLQ-LT). Each questionnaire has the same structure and consists of five sections: Section I – background; Section II – self-ratings of computing and digital skills; Section III – questions related to the use of digital technologies; Section IV – digital literacy test; and Section V – factors affecting the use of digital technologies for language learning and personal views on the use of digital devices. Look at the extract below and discuss how the questions, statements, and items of Section III can be updated to reflect recent digital pedagogies and digital technologies.

SECTION III

Q16. Please respond to each of the following questions by putting a tick (√) in the box at the appropriate spot: 'Yes' or 'No'.

		Yes	No
1	Do you understand the basic functions of computer hardware components?		
2	Do you have a personal homepage or a personal portfolio on the web?		
3	Do you use keyboard shortcuts?		
4	Do you use the computer for teaching purposes?		
5	Do you find it easy to learn something by reading it on the computer screen?		
6	Do you find it easy to learn something by watching it on the computer screen?		
7	Do you use social networking services?		
8	Do you have any online community you regularly visit?		
9	Do you feel competent in using digital teaching resources?		
10	Do you have mobile apps you use for language teaching purposes?		

Q17. Please respond to each of the following questions by putting a tick (√) in the box at the appropriate spot: 'Yes' or 'No'.

		Yes	No
1	Can you change computer screen brightness and contrast?		
2	Can you minimize, maximize and move windows on the computer screen?		
3	Can you use a 'search' command to locate a file?		
4	Can you scan disks for viruses?		
5	Can you write files onto a CD, a DVD or a USB drive?		
6	Can you create and update web pages?		
7	Can you take and edit digital photos?		
8	Can you record and edit digital sounds?		
9	Can you record and edit digital videos?		
10	Can you download and use apps on digital devices?		

Q18. Please indicate your level of frequency of using each of the followings by putting a tick (√) in the box at the appropriate spot: 'Very Frequently', 'Frequently', 'Occasionally', 'Rarely', 'Very Rarely' or 'Never'. If there is any item you do not know, it can be assumed that you do not have any experience with the item.

		Very Frequently	Frequently	Occasionally	Rarely	Very Rarely	Never
1	Word processor						
2	Email						
3	World Wide Web						
4	Graphics software						
5	Database						
6	Spreadsheet (for data organization)						

Continued....

		Very Frequently	Frequently	Occasionally	Rarely	Very Rarely	Never
7	Concordancer (for text analysis)						
8	Language learning software (CD-ROM, DVD)						
9	Language learning website						
10	Language learning mobile app						
11	Blog						
12	Wiki						
13	Text chatting						
14	Voice chatting						
15	Video conferencing						
16	Computer game						
17	Electronic dictionary						

Q19. How would you rate your skills for using each of the followings? Please put a tick (√) in the box at the appropriate spot: 'Very Good', 'Good', 'Acceptable', 'Poor', 'Very Poor', or 'Do Not Know'.

	Working with:	Very Good	Good	Acceptable	Poor	Very Poor	Do Not Know
1	Word processing applications (e.g., MS Word)						
2	Spreadsheet applications (e.g., MS Excel)						
3	Database applications (e.g., MS Access)						
4	Presentation applications (e.g., MS PowerPoint)						

Continued....

	Working with:	Very Good	Good	Acceptable	Poor	Very Poor	Do Not Know
5	Communication applications (e.g., Skype)						
6	Learning management systems (e.g., Moodle)						
7	Virtual worlds (e.g., Second Life)						
8	Social networking services (e.g., Facebook)						
9	Blogs (e.g., Blogger)						
10	Wikis (e.g., PBworks)						
11	Podcasts (e.g., Apple Podcasts)						
12	File sharing sites (e.g., Dropbox)						
13	Photo sharing sites (e.g., Picasa)						
14	Video sharing sites (e.g., YouTube)						
15	Web design applications (e.g., Dreamweaver)						
16	Web search engines (e.g., Google)						
17	Dictionary apps (e.g., Dictionary.com)						

Son (2015)

7.2 Digital pedagogies and digital technologies

Digital pedagogies and digital technologies should come together for digital language teaching. In their response to the question of what a digital pedagogy is, Howell and McMaster (2022) expressed the view that "a digital pedagogy is the study of how to teach using digital technologies to engage and empower students to become agents of their own learning" and asserted that "educators need to understand how to use technology effectively, understand the learning theories behind the practice, understand the impact of technology on learning, know how to select the right technology and decide when to use technology for the learning outcomes they seek" (p. 4). For the development of a digital pedagogy, they suggested that we need to develop "an attitude and aptitude that leads us to engage with new technologies as they emerge and look for their educational applications" (p. 9). With a focus on mediation, Kern (2015, 2018) called for a relational pedagogy with the five principles and pedagogical goals shown in Table 7.1. He emphasised the importance of mediation in the use of technology as follows:

> In language education, the use of technology should not be a goal in and of itself. Instead of thinking of technology only as a way to make learning more efficient, or more motivating, or more inclusive, or more culturally authentic, we ought also to consider ways of using technology to study the very ways it mediates language use, communication, cultural expression, and social meaning. That is, to adopt an approach that focuses on the very mediations that are part and parcel of all our communicative acts, and especially those that happen online, where our interpretations are significantly influenced by multiple layers of mediation. (Kern, 2015, pp. 258–259)

Models of digital pedagogies include blended learning, mobile learning, adaptive learning, personalised learning, and flipped classrooms (Carrier & Nye, 2017). Milton and Vozzo (2013) argued that the centre of digital pedagogies is co-construction of knowledge, including planning for learning, creating, editing, publishing online, and social networking. Based on the analysis of a set of publications, Santoveña-Casal and López (2023) contended that there was an expansion of digital pedagogy since 2016 with the development of interactive Web 4.0 and the impact of the COVID-19 pandemic on education. They called for more flexible pedagogies that can be adapted to different pedagogical scenarios.

It is important for language teachers to understand language learners' digital literacy practices. Williams et al. (2014) conducted a survey-based study on undergraduate foreign language students' use of digital tools and reported that a variety of factors (e.g., age, ownership of digital devices, digital skill levels, software availability) influenced the students' use of digital tools and digital literacy practices. In a telecollaboration project, Wu (2020) traced three Chinese EFL writers' digital literacy practices and found that the writers transferred literacy practices in response to their learning and communication needs in digital environments. In another EFL context, Kang and Kim (2021) examined factors affecting the quality of mobile-assisted digital-video-making task outcomes and reported that their students' English writing proficiency and first language narrative ability were significant predicting factors while digital literacy made no significant contribution to the quality of the task outcomes among the students who had a high level of digital literacy.

Table 7.1 *Principles and Pedagogical Goals of a Relational Pedagogy (adapted from Kern, 2015, p. 223)*

Principles	Pedagogical goals
1. Meanings are situated and relational, not autonomous.	Develop learners' awareness of how reframing and recontextualization affect meaning.
2. Language, literacy, and communication rely on both convention and invention.	Show learners the fundamental importance of social conventions in discourse, but also how people adapt conventions, resources, and designs for their individual and collective purposes.
3. The medium matters.	Encourage learners to reflect on how language forms are conventionally constrained by material contexts, and how they change over time. Familiarise them with historical precedents that have helped shaped the communication technologies they use. Develop their ability to analyse mediums critically for ideological or commercial underpinnings.
4. Texts and communication are always multimodal.	Encourage learners to reflect on how linguistic and non-linguistic elements interact in texts, as well as in face-to-face communication.
5. Language, technologies, and texts mediate between the social and the individual; between ourselves and real or imagined worlds.	Develop learners' awareness of this mediation and the consequences it can have for understanding. Get learners to think about how in the process of making texts they create social identities.

Price-Dennis et al. (2015) asserted that students' literacy practices and skills became more complex and deliberate by putting "a community of learners, digital tools, and real-world content" (p. 201) together. They concluded that the possibility for 21st century literacies to influence classroom discourse and digital learning experiences can be highlighted by situating the use of digital tools in classroom settings. Oskoz and Elora (2014) used a digital story development task in an advanced Spanish writing class, which aimed to enhance learners' digital skills. They reported that the integration of digital stories into the class "allowed learners to extend their knowledge of genres, grammar, and vocabulary; they also completed learning tasks that could foster personal creativity and practice with specific discourse structures" (p. 197). See Oskoz and Elora (2020) for a detailed discussion on digital L2 writing literacy practices. More recently, Yu and Zadorozhnyy (2022) explored the use of a video production project at an English-medium institution in Hong Kong and reported that the video presentation allowed their undergraduate students to develop their language, collaborative, and digital literacy skills. In Thailand, Waemusa and Jongwattanapaiboon (2023) investigated the use of mobile phones for developing EFL learners' digital literacies at Thai schools and reported that using mobile phones was not favoured at most schools. They emphasised the need for the effective use of mobile phones to promote digital literacies for English language learning in Thai school contexts.

Ortlieb et al. (2018) claimed that "collaboration across digital platforms promotes learning through crowd-accelerated learning, rhizomatic learning, citizen inquiry, massive open social learning, and even a maker culture" and said, "These approaches can foster genuine and relevant learning in teacher education programs, modernizing and matching instructional techniques with the teacher preparation demands of today and tomorrow" (p. 10). From a survey with college-level writing and communication teachers on digital resources they use, Robinson et al. (2019) found that the teachers performed a range of teaching tasks with both digital and non-digital tools and often relied on familiar or commonly available resources (e.g., learning management systems (LMSs), presentation software, email) for teacher and learner actions. They recommended the following actions:

1. Develop tailored training that supports teachers' self-reliance and incorporates a blend of digital and non-digital resources for teaching.
2. Develop a curated repository that compiles teachers' anecdotal experiences and experimental moments to provide a central collection to share and discuss digital resources.
3. Increase our involvement in the development of specific tools at all levels (e.g., as individual experts, as a field, and as organizations) so that tools are developed from pedagogical actions rather than trying to fit pedagogy around existing tools.
4. Create sustained, annual or biennial research studies to provide an ongoing, updated understanding of the ways the field uses digital resources. (pp. 14–15)

In another survey study of in-service EFL teachers' digital literacy, Cote and Milliner (2018) found that participants in the survey indicated that they were confident in using digital tools and pursuing advanced digital literacy skills. As their finding might not be congruent with other teachers in different contexts, there is still a strong need for teachers to develop digital literacy skills. Hockly (2015) argued that proving language teachers with necessary digital literacy skills could be carried out through "a careful consideration of training, teaching materials and technology" (p. 234). Regarding the relationship between foreign language teachers' digital literacy and self-efficacy, Kahveci (2021) found a positive correlation between the teachers' digital literacy and self-efficacy and reported that the amount of time spent online made a difference in their digital literacy and self-efficacy.

Considering online contexts for language learning, Cappellini and Combe (2022) discussed an orchestration of multiple online environments and asserted that teachers need the ability "to design tasks, tasks sequences, and scenarios while considering the affordances that arise from the relationships between environments" (p. 15). In a study of Turkish pre-service teachers' conceptualisation and practices of digital literacy, Akayoğlu et al. (2020) found that the pre-service teachers showed many levels of the concept of digital literacy and heavily used social media platforms such as *Facebook, Twitter, Instagram,* and *WhatsApp*. They pointed out the need for guiding the pre-service teachers' use of the platforms for their professional development.

Bilki et al. (2023), Hauck (2019), and Nicolaou (2021) suggested virtual exchange as a venue for digital literacy development. Bilki et al. (2023), in particular, analysed English language teachers' reflections on critical digital literacy as part of their virtual exchange experience and called for more closely guided and informed reflections on self-representation, inclusiveness, building connections, and social-political landscape. With a different focus, Shoecraft (2023) investigated the use of three digital tools (*Padlet, VoiceThread,* and *Microsoft Teams*) in Master of TESOL online courses and reported that the tools could enhance learning through increased motivation and participation, shared learning, and self-directed learning.

Based on Jones and Hafner's (2012) model of digital literacies, Hafner et al. (2015) presented five dimensions of digital literacies and example practices (see Table 7.2), which could be useful for language teachers to embed digital literacies in their language curriculum.

Table 7.2 *Dimensions of Digital Literacies and Example Practices (adapted from Hafner et al., 2015, pp. 2–3)*

Dimension	Focus	Example practices
Doing	Actions in the physical world	• Sharing pictures with friends • Searching for a place to eat online
Meaning	Forms of representation	• Posting to a social network site
Relating	Patterns of interaction	• Writing fan fiction for a massive online audience • Commenting on a blog post • Collaboratively writing an online article in a wiki
Thinking	Experiencing and thinking about reality	• Communicating through CMC • Participating in online affinity spaces
Being	Social identity	• Presenting oneself in a social network site • Adopting an expert role in an online (e.g., fan, gaming) community

Son (2020b) considered digital teaching strategies as "teaching plans and methods that are used to help learners achieve their learning goals with digital technologies" and stated that digital teaching strategies "need to be adapted to learners' needs and circumstances (e.g., time and devices available)" (p. 4). He reminded teachers to use the strategies appropriately:

> Teachers need to use a range of digital teaching strategies (e.g., exploration, identification, mind mapping, discussions, experiments, summarising, reinforcement, feedback, review, reflection) to increase learner engagement and active learning in digital environments. It is important for digital language teachers to employ appropriate digital language teaching strategies in their teaching contexts. (p. 4)

The following tips for integrating digital literacy into language teaching can be also of use to language teachers: identify and assess your students' digital proficiency levels; explore and choose digital tools that are appropriate for your students' needs and interests; provide clear instructions on how to use the digital tools for specific activities or tasks; model how to use the digital tools for language learning effectively; encourage your students to communicate and collaborate with each other using the digital tools; evaluate the effects of your digital literacy instruction on your student's learning outcomes; and keep reflecting on and improving your teaching practices with digital tools and resources.

In language learning and teaching, the use of digital tools has been widely discussed (e.g., Curwoord, 2011; Son, 2010, 2014b, 2023c; Wang et al., 2022; Wilden, 2013). There were also studies that investigated the effects of the use of digital tools on language learners' language skill development. For example, Levak and Son (2017) examined the effectiveness of the use of *Second Life* and *Skype* for developing listening comprehension and demonstrated how the digital tools could be used to facilitate interactions between learners of English or Croatian. In another study with Thai secondary school students, Wongsa and Son (2022) found that drama-based activities and *Facebook* had positive effects on the students' English-speaking skills, attitudes, and motivation in learning EFL. They reported that *Facebook*, as a social networking tool and a learning platform, increased communication and collaboration among the students.

Son's (2010) online tools for language teaching could be a good starting point for a discussion on the types of digital tools. As shown in Figure 7.2, he classified online tools for language teaching into twelve categories: learning/content management systems; communication tools; live and virtual worlds; social networking and bookmarking; blogs and wikis; presentation tools; resource sharing tools; website creation tools; web exercise creation tools; web search engines; dictionaries and concordancers; and utilities. Table 7.3 shows the list of digital tools updated from Son (2010) and adapted from Son (2023c).

Figure 7.2 *Categories of Online Tools for Language Teaching (Son, 2010)*

Table 7.3 *Online Tools for Language Teaching (adapted from Son, 2023c)*

1. Learning/Content Management Systems			
	Blackboard	https://www.blackboard.com/	Commercial LMS
	Canvas	https://www.canvaslms.com/	Open source LMS
	Drupal	https://www.drupal.org/	Open source CMS
	Joomla	https://www.joomla.org/	Open source CMS
	Moodle	https://moodle.org/	Open source LMS
	Sakai	https://www.sakaiproject.org/	Open source LMS
2. Communication Tools			
	Gmail	https://mail.google.com/	E-mail
	Skype	https://www.skype.com/	Chats
	Zoom	https://zoom.us/	Cloud-based video communication
	Cleverbot	https://www.cleverbot.com/	Chatbot
	MyBB	https://mybb.com/	Forum
	phpBB	https://www.phpbb.com/	Forum
3. Live and Virtual Worlds			
	ActiveWorlds	https://www.activeworlds.com/	3D virtual world
	Second Life	https://secondlife.com/	3D virtual world
	Twiddla	https://www.twiddla.com/	Virtual whiteboard
	WizIQ	https://www.wiziq.com/	Virtual classroom
4. Social Networking and Bookmarking			
	Diigo	https://www.diigo.com/	Social bookmarking
	Elgg	https://elgg.org/	Social networking
	Facebook	https://www.facebook.com/	Social networking
	Instagram	https://www.instagram.com/	Social networking
	MySpace	https://myspace.com/	Social networking
	Ning	https://www.ning.com/	Social networking
	LinkedIn	https://www.linkedin.com/	Professional network
	X	https://twitter.com/	Information network
	italki	https://www.italki.com/	Language learning community
	Lang-8	https://lang-8.com/	Language learning community

Continued....

Table 7.3 *Continued....*

5. Blogs and Wikis

Blogger	https://www.blogger.com/	Blog
Edublogs	https://edublogs.org/	Blog
LiveJournal	https://www.livejournal.com/	Blog & journal
WordPress.com	https://wordpress.com/	Blog
PBworks	https://www.pbworks.com/wikis.html	Wiki
Penzu	https://penzu.com/	Personal journal

6. Presentation Tools

Animoto	https://animoto.com/	Video slideshows
Canva	https://www.canva.com/	Graphic design
Pixton	https://www.pixton.com/	Comic and storyboard creator
Powtoon	https://www.powtoon.com/	Animated videos
Prezi	https://prezi.com/	Presentation editor
Renderforest	https://www.renderforest.com/	Animations and videos
Zoho Show	https://www.zoho.com/show/	Creating and sharing

7. Resource Sharing Tools

Google Docs	https://docs.google.com/	Documents
Zoho Writer	https://www.zoho.com/writer/	Documents
Box	https://www.box.com/	Files
Dropbox	https://www.dropbox.com/	Files
Google Drive	https://www.google.com/drive/	Files
VoiceThread	https://voicethread.com/	Group conversations
Flickr	https://www.flickr.com/	Photos
Google Photos	https://www.google.com/photos/	Photos
PodOmatic	https://www.podomatic.com/	Podcasts
Slideshare	https://www.slideshare.net/	Slides
SchoolTube	https://www.schooltube.com/	Videos
TeacherTube	https://www.teachertube.com/	Videos
VideoPress	https://videopress.com/	Videos
Vimeo	https://vimeo.com/	Videos
YouTube	https://www.youtube.com/	Videos

Continued....

Table 7.3 *Continued....*

8. Website Creation Tools

Google Sites	https://sites.google.com/	Pre-built templates
Jimdo	https://www.jimdo.com/	Website editor
Mahara	https://mahara.org/	E-portfolio system
Movable Type	https://movabletype.org/	Weblog management
SnapPages	https://snappages.com/	Drag-and-drop
Webnode	https://www.webnode.com/	Website builder
Webs	https://www.webs.com/	Website builder
Weebly	https://www.weebly.com/	Website builder
Wix	https://www.wix.com/	Website builder

9. Web Exercise Creation Tools

Baamboozle	https://www.baamboozle.com/	Classroom games
ClassMarker	https://www.classmarker.com/	Web-based test maker
ContentGenerator	https://www.contentgenerator.net/	Flash-based
EdPuzzle	https://edpuzzle.com/	Interactive videos
ESLVideo.com	https://eslvideo.com/	ESL video quizzes
JClic	https://clic.xtec.cat/legacy/en/jclic/	Java platform
Hot Potatoes	https://hotpot.uvic.ca/	JavaScript authoring
Kahoot!	https://kahoot.com/	Game-based classroom response system
Lingt	https://www.lingt.com/	Spoken exercises
Listen and Write	https://www.listen-and-write.com/	Dictation exercises
Online Quiz Creator	https://www.onlinequizcreator.com/	Playing or making quizzes for free
Quia	https://www.quia.com/	JavaScript authoring
Quizlet	https://quizlet.com/	Creating free flash-cards, games or quizzes
Quizizz	https://quizizz.com/	Online quizzes

Continued....

Table 7.3 *Continued....*

10. Web Search Engines

Ask.com	https://www.ask.com/	Ask Jeeves
Bing	https://www.bing.com/	Decision engine
DuckDuckGo	https://duckduckgo.com/	No tracking its users
Google	https://www.google.com/	PageRank
Yahoo! Search	https://search.yahoo.com/	Yahoo! Slurp

11. Dictionaries and Concordancers

Dictionary.com	https://www.dictionary.com/	Free online
Merriam-Webster Online	https://www.merriam-webster.com/	Free online
YourDictionary.com	https://www.yourdictionary.com/	Free online
Forvo	https://forvo.com/	Pronunciation dictionary
Howjsay	https://www.howjsay.com/	English pronunciation
Memrise	https://www.memrise.com/	Vocabulary learning
Visuwords	https://visuwords.com/	Graphical dictionary
OneLook Dictionary Search	https://www.onelook.com/	Dictionary search
British National Corpus	https://www.english-corpora.org/bnc/	English
Compleat Lexical Tutor	https://www.lextutor.ca/conc/	English and French

12. Utilities

Airtable	https://www.airtable.com/	Creating cloud spreadsheet-databases
CalculateMe	https://www.calculateme.com/	Conversion utility
Doodle	https://doodle.com/	Easy scheduling

Continued....

Table 7.3 *Continued....*

ClustrMaps	https://clustrmaps.com/	Monitoring website traffic
Currency Converter	https://www.oanda.com/currency/converter/	Currency calculator
Online converter	https://www.online-convert.com/	Converting media free
Google Earth	https://www.google.com/earth/	Virtual globe
Lesson Writer	https://www.lessonwriter.com/	Lesson plans
Lino	https://en.linoit.com/	Sticky notes
Storybird	https://storybird.com/	Collaborative storytelling
StoryJumper	https://www.storyjumper.com/	Creating storybooks
Cacoo	https://cacoo.com/	Collaborative diagramming
Mindmeister	https://www.mindmeister.com/	Mind mapping
Mindomo	https://www.mindomo.com/	Mind mapping
Popplet	https://www.popplet.com/	Mind mapping
Padlet	https://padlet.com/	Virtual wall
Remember the milk	https://www.rememberthemilk.com/	Task management
Remind	https://www.remind.com/	Text message reminders
SurveyMonkey	https://www.surveymonkey.com/	Online survey
Voki	https://www.voki.com/	Speaking avatar
Tiki-Toki	https://www.tiki-toki.com/	Timeline maker
Time and Date	https://www.timeanddate.com/	Time zones
TinyURL.com	https://tinyurl.com/	URL shortening
W3C Link Checker	https://validator.w3.org/checklink/	Links and anchors
Wayback Machine	https://archive.org/web/web.php	Internet archive
WordArt.com	https://wordart.com/	Word clouds
WordClouds.com	https://www.wordclouds.com/	Word clouds

Note: All web addresses are subject to change. You can use a search engine to locate it if you cannot find any particular website at the address given.

These tools can be recategorised in line with the five key elements of digital literacy as shown in Table 7.4. Teachers can use the tools to enhance language learners' learning experiences in digitally interactive environments.

Table 7.4 *Digital Tools Suggested for Five Key Elements of Digital Literacy*

Information search and evaluation	Ask.com (https://www.ask.com/)
	Bing (https://www.bing.com/)
	DuckDuckGo (https://duckduckgo.com/)
	Google (https://www.google.com/)
	Yahoo! Search (https://search.yahoo.com/)
Creation	Blogger (https://www.blogger.com/)
	Edublogs (https://edublogs.org/)
	LiveJournal (https://www.livejournal.com/)
	WordPress.com (https://wordpress.com/)
	Animoto (https://animoto.com/)
	Canva (https://www.canva.com/)
	Pixton (https://www.pixton.com/)
	Powtoon (https://www.powtoon.com/)
	Prezi (https://prezi.com/)
	Renderforest (https://www.renderforest.com/)
	Zoho Show (https://www.zoho.com/show/)
	Google Sites (https://sites.google.com/)
	Jimdo (https://www.jimdo.com/)
	Mahara (https://mahara.org/)
	Movable Type (https://movabletype.org/)
	SnapPages (https://snappages.com/)
	Webnode (https://www.webnode.com/)
	Webs (https://www.webs.com/)
	Weebly (https://www.weebly.com/)
	Wix (https://www.wix.com/)
	Baamboozle (https://www.baamboozle.com/)
	ClassMarker (https://www.classmarker.com/)
	ContentGenerator (https://www.contentgenerator.net/)
	EdPuzzle (https://edpuzzle.com/)
	ESLVideo.com (https://eslvideo.com/)
	JClic (https://clic.xtec.cat/legacy/en/jclic/)
	Hot Potatoes (https://hotpot.uvic.ca/)
	Kahoot! (https://kahoot.com/)
	Lingt (https://www.lingt.com/)
	Listen and Write (https://www.listen-and-write.com/)
	Online Quiz Creator (https://www.onlinequizcreator.com/)

Continued....

Table 7.4 *Continued....*

	Quia (https://www.quia.com/)
	Quizlet (https://quizlet.com/)
	Quizizz (https://quizizz.com)
	Airtable (https://www.airtable.com/)
	Storybird (https://storybird.com/)
	StoryJumper (https://www.storyjumper.com/)
	WordArt.com (https://wordart.com/)
	WordClouds.com (https://www.wordclouds.com/)
Communication	Gmail (https://mail.google.com/)
	Skype (https://www.skype.com/)
	Zoom (https://zoom.us/)
	Cleverbot (https://www.cleverbot.com/)
	MyBB (https://mybb.com/)
	phpBB (https://www.phpbb.com/)
	ActiveWorlds (https://www.activeworlds.com/)
	Second Life (https://secondlife.com/)
	Elgg (https://elgg.org/)
	Facebook (https://www.facebook.com/)
	Instagram (https://www.instagram.com/)
	MySpace (https://myspace.com/)
	Ning (https://www.ning.com/)
	LinkedIn (https://www.linkedin.com/)
	X (https://twitter.com/)
Collaboration	Diigo (https://www.diigo.com/)
	italki (https://www.italki.com/)
	Lang-8 (https://lang-8.com/)
	PBworks (https://www.pbworks.com/wikis.html)
	Cacoo (https://cacoo.com/)
	Mindmeister (https://www.mindmeister.com/)
	Mindomo (https://www.mindomo.com/)
	Popplet (https://www.popplet.com/)
	Padlet (https://padlet.com/)
Online safety	Google Docs (https://docs.google.com/)
	Zoho Writer (https://www.zoho.com/writer/)
	Box (https://www.box.com/)
	Dropbox (https://www.dropbox.com/)
	Google Drive (https://www.google.com/drive/)
	VoiceThread (https://voicethread.com/)
	Flickr (https://www.flickr.com/)
	Google Photos (https://www.google.com/photos/)

Continued....

Table 7.4 *Continued....*

PodOmatic (https://www.podomatic.com/)
SlideShare (https://www.slideshare.net/)
SchoolTube (https://www.schooltube.com/)
TeacherTube (https://www.teachertube.com/)
VideoPress (https://videopress.com/)
Vimeo (https://vimeo.com/)
YouTube (https://www.youtube.com/)

Note: These example tools can be listed in more than one category due to their integrated features.

In terms of types of language learning activities, Richards and Lockhart (1996) categorised the types into: presentation activities (to introduce and clarify a new learning item); practice activities (to perform or learn an item that has been previously presented); memorisation activities (to memorise information or learning items); comprehension activities (to develop or demonstrate the understanding of written or spoken texts); application activities (to creatively use knowledge and skills that have been previously presented and practiced); strategy activities (to develop particular learning strategies and approaches to learning); affective activities (to develop students' interest, confidence, and positive attitudes toward learning); feedback activities (to give feedback on learning or performance); and assessment activities (to evaluate the extent to which the goals of an activity or lesson have been accomplished). In selecting and designing language learning activities, they suggested to ask and check the following questions related to dimension of activities such as purposes, procedures, sequencing, complexity, resources, grouping, strategies, language, timing, outcomes, and assessment:

> How will the purposes of an activity be communicated to the students?
> What procedures will students use in completing an activity?
> How will the activity be sequenced in relation to other activities within the same lesson?
> What kinds of demands does the activity make on learners?
> What resources will be required?
> What grouping arrangements will be used?
> Should a particular learning strategy be used in carrying out an activity?
> What language or language learning focus should the activity have?
> How much time should students spend on the activity?

What will the outcome of the activity be?
How will student performance on the activity be
assessed? (pp. 167–172)

These questions could be equally useful when we design digital language learning activities. It would be also helpful for teachers to use a planner for each digital literacy activity as part of a lesson plan (see Table 7.5 for an example digital literacy activity planner).

Table 7.5 *Example Digital Activity Planner*

Date	
Class	
Activity Title	
Activity Objectives	
Target Language	
Target Language Skills & Areas	
Learner Levels	
Activity Length	
Preparation Time	
Components of Digital Literacy Aiming to Support	
Technical Requirements & Resources	
Teacher Role	
Procedure	
Options & Suggestions	

Chapter 7

Son (2017, 2023d) presented a list of fourteen types of online activities for language learning (i.e., collaboration; communication; concordancing; creation; exploration; games; mapping; presentation; reflection; simulation; storytelling; surveys; tests; and tutorials) together with example online tools that can be used for each activity type. Table 7.6 shows some example tools that are suggested for creation, communication, and collaboration.

Table 7.6 *Online Activities for Language Learning (adapted from Son, 2023d)*

Activity Types	Example Activities	Example Tools
Creation	Books	Book Creator (https://bookcreator.com/)
	Databases	Airtable (https://www.airtable.com/)
	Diagrams	Cacoo (https://nulab.com/cacoo/)
	ePortfolios	Mahara (https://mahara.org/)
	Graphics	Canva (https://www.canva.com/)
	Podcasts	PodOmatic (https://www.podomatic.com/)
	Videos	Animato (https://animoto.com/); Renderforest (https://www.renderforest.com/)
	Websites	Google Sites (https://sites.google.com/); Webnode (https://www.webnode.com/); Weebly (https://www.weebly.com/); Wix (https://www.wix.com/)
	Word clouds	WordArt.com (https://wordart.com/); WordClouds.com (https://www.wordclouds.com/)
Communication	Email	Gmail (https://mail.google.com/)
	Forums	MyBB (https://mybb.com/)
	Social networking	Facebook (https://www.facebook.com/)
	Video chats	Skype (https://www.skype.com/); Zoom (https://zoom.us/)
Collaboration	Real-time editing	Etherpad (https://etherpad.org/)
	Social bookmarking	Diigo (https://www.diigo.com/)
	Virtual communities	Italki (https://www.italki.com/); Lang-8 (https://lang-8.com/)
	Wikis	PBworks (https://www.pbworks.com/wikis.html)

Example Activity

The example activity (Son, 2020c) below demonstrates how digital tools can be used for MALL in an English for academic purposes (EAP) context.

Activity Title	Mobile-assisted academic vocabulary learning
Introduction	English for academic purposes (EAP) students need to increase their academic vocabulary knowledge for their academic success. This activity provides EAP students with formal and informal mobile-assisted language learning opportunities to learn selected words from Son's (2019) Academic English Word List (AEWL).
Target Language	English
Target Language Skills & Areas	Reading; vocabulary
Learner Levels	EAP students; Intermediate – advanced
Activity Aims	This activity aims to help students develop and improve their academic vocabulary knowledge through online language learning activities on mobile devices.
Activity Length	40 minutes; variable
Preparation Time	60 minutes; time for the teacher to select words from the AEWL and create a study set on *Quizlet* and a series of multiple-choice questions on *Kahoot!* with the selected words
Technical Requirements & Resources	A teacher computer with a projector; a mobile device (e.g., a smartphone, a tablet, a laptop) for each student; *Quizlet* (https://quizlet.com/); *Kahoot!* (https://kahoot.com/)
Procedure	1. Introduce the online tools and activities to the students. Consider learner training if needed. 2. Implement a sample activity with *Quizlet* and *Kahoot!*. 3. Invite the students to ask any questions. 4. Guide the students how to use the learning activities on *Quizlet* (for self-study) and *Kahoot!* (homework challenge mode for self-testing). 5. Discuss mobile-assisted vocabulary learning with the students. 6. Encourage the students to use the online activities out of the classroom. 7. Check the students' progress regularly. 8. Test the students with *Kahoot!* after a certain period of time.

Continued....

Example Activity *Continued....*

Options and Suggestions	• For activity design, the teacher needs to consider contents, tools, and activity types. • For activity implementation, the teacher needs to consider learner training, ways of integrating into classroom activities, mobile learning, and tracking learner progress. • The teacher can encourage the students to reflect their experiences with *Quizlet* and *Kahoot!* in online discussion forums.
Justification	Academic vocabulary is a key component of academic success. The value of academic vocabulary lists for direct teaching is widely accepted (Coxhead, 2000; Gardner & Davies, 2014; Paquot, 2010). Previous research (e.g., Azabdaftari & Mozaheb, 2012; Chen, Liu, & Huang, 2019; Dizon, 2016) also indicates that mobile-assisted language learning (MALL) is useful for vocabulary learning. A range of online activities can be created by using a variety of online tools (Son, 2010) and used with mobile devices in and out of the classroom (Son, 2016). In this activity, *Quizlet* and *Kahoot!* are used to create mobile-assisted vocabulary learning activities with words from Son's (2019) AEWL, which serves as an academic vocabulary resource for EAP students. The activity offers the students opportunities to improve their academic vocabulary knowledge anytime and anywhere. It also encourages teachers to consider MALL and online learning activities (e.g., Son, 2017) containing context-specific vocabulary.
References and Further Reading	Azabdaftari, B., & Mozaheb, M. A. (2012). Comparing vocabulary learning of EFL learners by using two different strategies: Mobile learning vs. flashcards. *The EUROCALL Review, 20*(2), 47-59. https://polipapers.upv.es/index.php/eurocall/article/view/11377 Chen, C.-M., Liu, H., & Huang, H.-B. (2019). Effects of a mobile game-based English vocabulary learning app on learners' perceptions and learning performance: A case study of Taiwanese EFL learners. *ReCALL, 31*(2), 170-188. https://doi.org/10.1017/S0958344018000228

Continued....

Example Activity *Continued....*

> Coxhead, A. (2000). A new academic word list. *TESOL Quarterly, 34*(2), 213–238. https://doi.org/10.2307/3587951
>
> Dizon, G. (2016). Quizlet in the EFL classroom: Enhancing academic vocabulary acquisition of Japanese University students. *Teaching English with Technology, 16*(2), 40-56. http://www.tewtjournal.org/?wpdmact=process&did=NDQzLmhvdGxpbms
>
> Gardner, D., & Davies, M. (2014). A new academic vocabulary list. *Applied Linguistics, 35*(3), 305-327. https://doi.org/10.1093/applin/amt015
>
> Paquot, M. (2010). *Academic vocabulary in learner writing: From extraction to analysis.* Continuum International.
>
> Son, J.-B. (2010). Online tools for language teaching. http://drjbson.com/projects/tools/
>
> Son, J.-B. (2016). Selecting and evaluating mobile apps for language learning. In A. Palalas & M. Ally (Eds.), *The international handbook of mobile-assisted language learning* (pp. 161–179). China Central Radio & TV University Press. http://drjbson.com/papers/MALL_Ch6_JS_2016.pdf
>
> Son, J.-B. (2017). Online activities for language learning. http://drjbson.com/projects/oall/
>
> Son, J.-B. (2019). Academic English word list. http://drjbson.com/projects/aewl/
>
> Son, J.-B. (2019). Learner training in digital language learning for pre-service translators and interpreters. In J.-B. Son (Ed.), *Context-specific computer-assisted language learning: Research, development and practice* (pp. 27–49). APACALL. http://www.apacall.org/research/books/4/

(Son, 2020c, pp. 18–21)

Task 7.2a

Which three digital tools do you use most for language learning/teaching? Name them and describe how you use them.

Task 7.2b

Create a digital portfolio that showcases your digital literacy skills and technology integration in language teaching and includes examples of language lesson plans, learning activities, and assessments using digital tools and resources.

Task 7.2c

There are many studies on informal digital language learning (e.g., Lee, 2019, 2022; Zhang & Liu, 2023). What strategies can you use to encourage students' self-directed learning in extramural contexts?

7.3 Developing digital language teaching skills

Digital language teaching skills empower language teachers to integrate digital pedagogies and digital technologies into language instruction and involve the use of various digital tools and resources for language learning. They are crucial for maximising language learning in digital environments where language skills (i.e., reading, writing, listening, and speaking) need to be expanded to multimodal skills. Hafner (2014) argued that the scope of English language teaching should be "expanded beyond the traditional focus on speech and writing to the production of multimodal ensembles, drawing on a range of other semiotic modes" (p. 655).

Redecker (2017) presented a European Framework for the Digital Competence of Educators (DigCompEdu), which was directed toward educators at all levels of education. The framework consists of the following six areas: (1) professional engagement (using digital technologies for communication, collaboration and professional development); (2) digital resources (sourcing, creating and sharing digital resources); (3) teaching and learning (managing and orchestrating the use of digital technologies in teaching and learning); (4) assessment (using digital technologies and strategies to enhance assessment); (5) empowering learners (using digital technologies to enhance inclusion, personalisation and learners' active engagement); and (6) facilitating learners' digital competence (enabling learners to creatively and responsibly use digital technologies for information, communication, content creation, wellbeing and problem-solving).

In the DigCompEdu framework, each area includes different competences as follows:

Area 1. Professional engagement: organisational communication; professional collaboration; reflective practice; digital continuous professional development

Area 2. Digital resources: selecting digital resources; creating and modifying digital resources; managing, protecting, and sharing digital resources

Area 3. Teaching and learning: teaching; guidance; collaborative learning; self-regulated learning

Area 4. Assessment: assessment strategies; analysing evidence; feedback and planning

Area 5. Empowering learners: accessibility and inclusion; differentiation and personalisation; actively engaging learners

Area 6. Facilitating learners' digital competence: information and media literacy; digital communication and collaboration; digital content creation; responsible use; digital problem solving   (p. 16)

In terms of proficiency levels of educators, the framework describes six stages: Newcomer, Explorer, Integrator, Expert, Leader, and Pioneer. In teaching, for example, each level has different proficiency statements as follows:

- Newcomer: I do not or only very rarely use digital devices or digital content in my teaching.
- Explorer: I use available classroom technologies, e.g., digital whiteboards, projectors, PCs. I choose digital technologies according to the learning objective and context.
- Integrator: I organise and manage the integration of digital devices (e.g., classroom technologies, students' devices) into the teaching and learning process. I manage the integration of digital content, e.g., videos, interactive activities, into the teaching and learning process.
- Expert: I consider appropriate social settings and interaction modes when integrating digital technologies. I use digital technologies in teaching to increase methodological variation. I set up learning sessions or other interactions in a digital environment.

- Leader: I structure learning sessions so that different (teacher-led and learner-led) digital activities jointly reinforce the learning objective. I structure and manage content, contributions and interaction in a digital environment. I continuously evaluate the effectiveness of digitally enhanced teaching strategies and revise my strategies accordingly.
- Pioneer: I provide full courses or learning modules in a digital learning environment. I experiment with and develop new formats and pedagogical methods for instruction. (Redecker, 2017, p. 53)

In digital problem solving, on the other hand, the following proficiency statements are given for each level:

- Newcomer: I do not or only very rarely consider how to foster learners' digital problem solving.
- Explorer: I encourage learners to solve technical problems using trial and error. I encourage learners to transfer their digital competence to new situations.
- Integrator: I implement learning activities in which learners use digital technologies creatively, expanding their technical repertoire. I encourage learners to help each other in developing their digital competence.
- Expert: I use a range of different pedagogic strategies to enable learners to apply their digital competence to new situations or in new contexts. I encourage learners to reflect on the limits of their digital competence and help them identify suitable strategies for further developing it.
- Leader: I enable learners to seek out different technological solutions to a problem, investigate their benefits and drawback, and critically and creatively come up with a new solution or product. I critically reflect on the suitability of my pedagogic strategies to foster learners' digital competence, expand their repertoire of digital strategies, and adapt my methods accordingly.
- Pioneer: I enable learners to apply their digital competence in unconventional ways to new situations and creatively come up with new solutions or products. I reflect on, discuss, re-design, and innovate pedagogic strategies for fostering learners' digital problem solving skills. (Redecker, 2017, p. 87)

Built on Janssen et al.'s (2013) work, on the other hand, Falloon (2020) presented a teacher digital competence framework, which extended Mishra and Koehler's (2006) technological pedagogical and content knowledge (TPACK) competences and contained two sets of integrated competencies: personal-ethical competencies (awareness, concern, action) and personal-professional competencies (operational). In his framework, he showed "the importance of teacher education students understanding how to integrate into subject-related activities involving learning with, about and through digital technologies, understandings and capabilities aligned with personal-ethical and personal-professional competencies" (p. 2462).

Language teachers need digital competence underpinned by knowledge, attitudes, skills, and strategies necessary for digital language teaching. They can develop their digital language teaching skills through digital literacy practices that foster ICCCO and facilitate engagement with the use of digital tools, dynamic resources, and learning activities. They can use professional development opportunities (e.g., workshops, seminars, conferences, courses, communities of practice), which can be taken as formal learning and/or informal learning (Son, 2018). With regard to online reflection, for instance, Farrell (2018) stated that "language teachers are increasingly participating in online reflective communities for their professional development" (pp. 221–222) and added, "Such online communities are said to provide teachers with supportive and collaborative reflective discussions in which they can share teaching techniques, and explore new ways of teaching as well as pursue their individual interest related to their own professional development" (p. 222). In Canada, Beach et al. (2021) reviewed 11 studies of online teacher professional development published between 2000 and 2020 and identified four themes: knowledge exchange, reflective practice, multifaceted learning opportunities; and just-in-time support. They highlighted research needs to examine online teacher professional development across diverse regions.

Adapted from the La Trobe University Digital Literacies Framework Reference Group (2019), the following digital capabilities can be suggested for language teachers to be able to: demonstrate how to use digital tools and resources for educational purposes; set up digital activities for students to undertake independently and/or in collaboration (e.g., online quizzes, simulations, presentations, voting, building wiki pages, collating online resources, webinars); set up online peer review and feedback; set up and deliver online assessments; design online materials relevant to students' learning needs; use diagnostic tools to better understand students' learning processes and outcomes; use online learning platforms or management systems to create learning opportunities and deliver learning resources; use digital tools to record learning events or data and analyse them for reflective teaching; provide access to authentic and engaging content relevant and appropriate to students' language levels; provide feedback to students in digital formats accessible and actionable; provide an interactive, engaging, and personalised learning experience with an appropriate combination of digital tools and resources; provide a blended learning experience with a strategic mix of online and face-to-face activities; incorporate innovative pedagogical approaches to language teaching; facilitate and support online discussions; help students develop a deeper understanding of the target language and culture through digital creation, communication, and collaboration; and encourage and manage motivation to learn in digital settings.

For the successful implementation of digital language teaching, language teachers need to have the ability to understand how digital technologies work and use digital tools effectively, responsibly, and ethically. They also need to keep up to date with the rapid development of digital technology through continuing professional development in technology-enhanced language teaching (TELT). Son (2021) reviewed technology standards for teachers, which provide "guidance for technology use" (p. 6) and discussed several professional development frameworks for teachers, which provide "a set of competencies and activities that teachers need to have in learning and teaching" (p. 6). The Cambridge English Digital Framework for Language Teachers developed by Cambridge Assessment English (2017), for example, has six categories of digital professional development: the digital world; the digital classroom; the digital teacher; designing learning; delivering learning; and evaluating learning. In the digital teacher category, specifically, the framework guides teachers to get involved in reflection and development with digital tools and resources and share knowledge and best practice through a professional community. Another guide for professional development in digital language teaching is Son's (2020b) Digital Language Teacher Development Framework (DLTDF). He stated that "the framework is intended to support language teachers to identify what they can do and how they can engage with its four interrelated components: exploration, communication, collaboration and reflection" (p. 6). Table 7.7 presents the framework showing key activities connected with ECCR and Table 7.8 presents a description of three competency levels of the framework.

Table 7.7 *Digital Language Teacher Development Framework (DLTDF) (Son, 2020b, pp. 7–8)*

	Components			
	Exploration	Communication	Collaboration	Reflection
Activities	• Collect information on digital technologies, tools and resources • Learn about computer-assisted language learning (CALL) • Learn how to use digital technologies in the classroom • Trial new technologies	• Interact with learners, colleagues, administrators, other practitioners, teacher educators and researchers • Use computer-mediated communication (CMC) tools to interact with others personally, socially and professionally • Develop online communication skills	• Work together with others in professional communities • Share information, experiences, ideas and resources with other teachers • Plan, design and manage collaborative activities • Facilitate collaboration with online communication tools	• Examine experiences critically • Reflect on one's own learning and teaching practices • Think and practice reflectively • Do self-monitoring • Engage with critical and contextualized reflection
Sample Questions for Self-Assessment	1. Are you active in collecting information on technological options for your teaching? If yes, how do you collect the information and how does the information affect your pedagogy? If no, why not?	1. What communication skills and strategies do you think are needed in increasing student interaction during online learning activities?	1. What do you think about working in a team environment for online learning activities?	1. What are the challenges of using digital tools in your teaching context?

2. What factors do you think are important in the selection of digital tools for your teaching?

2. How do you build and maintain your communication channels with other professionals?

2. How do you think you can collaborate with your colleagues and students online?

2. Do you consider yourself a teacher who is competent in technology-enhanced language teaching (TELT)? If yes, how do you see your role in the technology-enhanced language classroom? If no, why not? Any plan for TELT?

Table 7.8 Competency Levels of the Digital Language Teacher Development Framework (Son, 2020b, pp. 8–9)

	Beginner (a novice knowledge and skill level)	Intermediate (between a beginner and an expert)	Expert (a highly developed knowledge and skill level)
Exploration	• I am little active in collecting information on technological options for teaching. • I have limited knowledge and skills for selecting useful digital tools for my teaching.	• I am reasonably active in collecting information on technological options for teaching. • I have reasonable knowledge and skills for selecting useful digital tools for my teaching.	• I am very active in collecting information on technological options for teaching. • I have advanced knowledge and skills for selecting useful digital tools for my teaching.
Communication	• I have a basic understanding of online communication skills and strategies for increasing student interaction. • I have little knowledge of and experience in building and maintaining communication channels with other professionals.	• I have a reasonable understanding of online communication skills and strategies for increasing student interaction. • I have reasonable knowledge of and experience in building and maintaining communication channels with other professionals.	• I have a well-developed understanding of online communication skills and strategies for increasing student interaction. • I have advanced knowledge of and experience in building and maintaining communication channels with other professionals.

Collaboration	• I have a basic understanding of working in a team in a digital environment. • I can collaborate with my colleagues and students online in a limited way.	• I have a reasonable understanding of working in a team in a digital environment. • I can collaborate with my colleagues and students online in a reasonable way.	• I have a well-developed understanding of working in a team in a digital environment. • I can collaborate with my colleagues and students online in a highly productive way.
Reflection	• I can reflect on my teaching with digital technologies in a limited way. • I have a basic understanding of self-monitoring in digital contexts.	• I can reflect on my teaching with digital technologies in a reasonable way. • I have a reasonable understanding of self-monitoring in digital contexts.	• I can reflect on my teaching with digital technologies in a highly efficient way. • I have a well-developed understanding of self-monitoring in digital contexts.

Teachers are encouraged to engage with various ongoing professional development activities and increase their knowledge and skills for digital language teaching (Son, 2021). The demand for digitally competent teachers needs to be addressed with new approaches to technology integration in teacher education (Instefjord & Munthe, 2017). In language teacher education programs, teacher educators need to carefully consider how to plan and deliver digital literacy training for language teachers, which can guide and support teachers to develop and improve their digital competence in designing, implementing, and evaluating language learning activities using digital tools and resources, while considering personal and professional connections in multilingual and multimodal online communities. Teacher educators are recommended to explore multidimensional aspects (e.g., theoretical aspects, pedagogical aspects, technological aspects, socio-cultural aspects, practical aspects) of digital literacy and demonstrate what and how digital language teaching activities can be used/adapted in digital environments. It is hoped that the ideas presented in this book facilitate and stimulate discussion and innovation on the effective ways of developing and improving teacher competencies in digital language teaching.

Task 7.3a

Ng et al. (2023) pointed out a growing need for teachers to equip with AI competencies and Son et al. (2023) recommended teachers to be prepared to use AI technologies and applications effectively. Discuss what support and resources you think teachers need in order to develop digital competencies in AI-powered learning environments.

Task 7.3b

The Digital Tool Evaluation Form below guides you a thorough evaluation of the affordances of a digital tool for digital language teaching. Your task is to use the criteria given in the form to assess a specific digital tool/resource to use in your teaching. Your evaluation can help you understand and decide whether the digital tool can meet your needs. Discuss the results of the evaluation with your colleagues.

Digital Tool Evaluation Form

Digital Tool Information	
Name	
Place (web address) to download/use	
Price	
Last updated date	
Version	
Size	
Publisher/developer	
Target audience	
Language activities/skills to practice	☐ Reading ☐ Writing ☐ Listening ☐ Speaking ☐ Vocabulary ☐ Grammar ☐ Pronunciation ☐ Culture ☐ None ☐ Other – Please specify:
Short description	

Digital Tool Evaluation

1. Accessibility: Is it easy to access? Is it freely available? Is it a value for money if it is a paid version?

Very Unsatisfactory	Unsatisfactory	Neutral/ Uncertain	Satisfactory	Very Satisfactory

2. Navigation: Is it easy to navigate? Does it provide clear directions?

Very Unsatisfactory	Unsatisfactory	Neutral/ Uncertain	Satisfactory	Very Satisfactory

3. Reliability: Is it reliable? Does it perform without technical issues?

Very Unsatisfactory	Unsatisfactory	Neutral/ Uncertain	Satisfactory	Very Satisfactory

4. Design: Does it look friendly? Is it organised logically? Does it make effective use of multimedia?

Very Unsatisfactory	Unsatisfactory	Neutral/ Uncertain	Satisfactory	Very Satisfactory

5. Features: Does it offer useful features? Does it take advantage of digital technologies?

Very Unsatisfactory	Unsatisfactory	Neutral/ Uncertain	Satisfactory	Very Satisfactory

6. Usefulness: Is it useful for learning? Does it provide practical learning activities?

Very Unsatisfactory	Unsatisfactory	Neutral/ Uncertain	Satisfactory	Very Satisfactory

7. Engagement: Does it provide an engaging experience? Does it provide reinforcement to hold the interest of users? Does it offer a meaningful and interactive learning environment?

Very Unsatisfactory	Unsatisfactory	Neutral/ Uncertain	Satisfactory	Very Satisfactory

8. Flexibility: Is it flexible to adapt to user needs? Can it be used for different types of activities? Does it offer opportunities to collaborate with others?

Very Unsatisfactory	Unsatisfactory	Neutral/ Uncertain	Satisfactory	Very Satisfactory

9. Feedback: Does it provide options for feedback and performance data? Is its feedback constructive and timely?

Very Unsatisfactory	Unsatisfactory	Neutral/ Uncertain	Satisfactory	Very Satisfactory

10. Security: Does it utilise an effective security policy and technology to protect user privacy and confidentiality?

Very Unsatisfactory	Unsatisfactory	Neutral/ Uncertain	Satisfactory	Very Satisfactory

11. Support: Is user assistance available? Is online help adequate? Does it provide necessary updates?

Very Unsatisfactory	Unsatisfactory	Neutral/ Uncertain	Satisfactory	Very Satisfactory

12. Integration: Can it be connected to a curriculum? Does the use of the tool fit with teaching goals?

Very Unsatisfactory	Unsatisfactory	Neutral/ Uncertain	Satisfactory	Very Satisfactory

Overall Rating

_____ 1 Very Poor (Not recommended at all)
_____ 2 Poor (Not appropriate)
_____ 3 Adequate (Acceptable with reservation)
_____ 4 Good (Appropriate for use)
_____ 5 Excellent (Highly recommended)

Additional Comments

Reviewer		Date reviewed	

Discussion Questions

1. What do you think digital literacy education should consist of?
2. What do you think the role of teachers is in digital language classrooms?
3. How can digital tools enhance the development of multimodal skills?
4. How can we teach language learners to be digitally literate and competent?

5. How can we effectively use digital tools and resources in language lessons?
6. How can we effectively integrate digital literacy into second/foreign/additional language teaching?
7. What do you think about professional learning in digital language teaching?
8. What do you like to see in digital literacy training for language teachers?
9. How do you think informal learning might contribute to the development of digital literacy?
10. What do you think the most important consideration is when designing a digital language learning activity for your students?
11. What challenges do you have in digital language teaching in your context?
12. What strategies do you employ to respond to the challenges?

References

Adelore, O. O. & Ojedeji, S. O. (2022). Digital literacy: Key to equity and social justice in a tech-dependent world. In P. A. Robinson, K. V. Williams & M. Stojanović (Eds.), *Global citizenship for adult education: Advancing critical literacies for equity and social justice* (pp. 316–324). Routledge.

Akayoğlu, S., Satar, H. M., Dikilitaş, K., Cirit, N. C., & Korkmazgil, S. (2020). Digital literacy practices of Turkish pre-service EFL teachers. *Australasian Journal of Educational Technology, 36*(1), 85–97. https://doi.org/10.14742/ajet.4711

Albert, S., Flournoy, D., & LeBrasseur, R. (2009). *Networked communities: Strategies for digital collaboration*. Information Science Reference.

Ally, M. (2019). Competency profile of the digital and online teacher in future education. *International Review of Research in Open and Distributed Learning, 20*(2), 302–318. https://doi.org/10.19173/irrodl.v20i2.4206

Alm, A. (2020). L2 chat for semi-formal and informal language learning. In J.-B. Son (Ed.), *Technology-enhanced language teaching in action* (pp. 38–41). APACALL. https://www.apacall.org/research/books/5/

Andretta, S. (2005). From prescribed reading to the excitement or the burden of choice: Information literacy: Foundation of e-learning. *Aslib Proceedings, 57*(2), 181–190. https://doi.org/10.1108/00012530510589146

Andujar, A., & Nadif, F. Z. (2022). Evaluating an inclusive blended learning environment in EFL: A flipped approach. *Computer Assisted Language Learning, 35*(5–6), 1138–1167. https://doi.org/10.1080/09588221.2020.1774613

Anwaruddin, S. M. (2019). Teaching language, promoting social justice: A dialogic approach to using social media. *CALICO Journal, 36*(1), 1–18. https://doi.org/10.1558/cj.35208

Aoki, K. & Molnar, P. (2011). Project-based international collaborative learning using web 2.0 tools for authentic learning of foreign language and 21st century skills. In T. Bastiaens & M. Ebner (Eds.), *Proceedings of ED-MEDIA 2011 – World Conference on Educational Multimedia, Hypermedia & Telecommunications* (pp. 2349–2353). Association for the Advancement of Computing in Education (AACE). https://www.learntechlib.org/primary/p/38186/

Australian Curriculum, Assessment and Reporting Authority (ACARA). (2021). *Australian curriculum review: General capabilities – Digital literacy*. https://www.australiancurriculum.edu.au/media/7024/gc_digital_literacy_ict_capability_consultation_curriculum.pdf

Bacalja, A., Beavis, C., & O'Brien, A. (2022). Shifting landscapes of digital literacy. *The Australian Journal of Language and Literacy, 45*, 253–263. https://doi.org/10.1007/s44020-022-00019-x

Barrot, J. S. (2022). Social media as a language learning environment: A systematic review of the literature (2008–2019). *Computer Assisted Language Learning, 35*(9), 2534–2562. https://doi.org/10.1080/09588221.2021.1883673

Beach, P., Favret, E., & Minuk, A. (2021). Online teacher professional development in Canada: A review of the research. *Canadian Journal of Learning and Technology, 47*(2), 1–23. https://doi.org/10.21432/cjlt27948

Belshaw, D. (2014). *The essential elements of digital literacies.* https://dougbelshaw.com/essential-elements-book.pdf

Bennett, M. J. (1993). Towards ethnorelativism: A developmental model of intercultural sensitivity. In R. M. Paige (Ed.), *Education for the intercultural experience* (pp. 21–71). Intercultural Press.

Bensal, E. R. (2023). Creating an academic poster. In J.-B. Son (Ed.), *Online language teaching in action* (pp. 48–51). APACALL. https://www.apacall.org/research/books/7/

Benson, P. (2017). *The discourse of YouTube: Multimodal text in a global context.* Routledge.

Bigelow, S. J. (2022). Data privacy (information privacy). *Teach Target.* https://www.techtarget.com/searchcio/definition/data-privacy-information-privacy

Bilki, Z., Satar, M., & Sak, M. (2023). Critical digital literacy in virtual exchange for ELT teacher education: An interpretivist methodology. *ReCALL, 35*(1), 58–73. https://doi.org/10.1017/S095834402200009X

Buckingham, D. (2015). Defining digital literacy: What do young people need to know about digital media? *Nordic Journal of Digital Literacy, 10*(Jubileumsnummer Issue), 21–34. https://doi.org/10.18261/ISSN1891-943X-2015-Jubileumsnummer-03

Bui, T. H. (2022). English teachers' integration of digital technologies in the classroom. *International Journal of Educational Research Open, 3*, 100204. https://doi.org/10.1016/j.ijedro.2022.100204

Byram, M. (1997). *Teaching and assessing intercultural communicative competence.* Multilingual Matters.

Calvani, A., Cartelli, A., Fini, A., & Ranieri, M. (2008). Models and instruments for assessing digital competence at school. *Journal of e-Learning and Knowledge Society, 4*(3), 183–193. https://doi.org/10.20368/1971-8829/288

Cambridge Assessment English. (2017). *The Cambridge English digital framework for language teachers.* Cambridge Assessment English. https://thedigitalteacher.com/framework

Campbell, A. (2023). Using digitally shared student-generated questions. In J.-B. Son (Ed.), *Online language teaching in action* (pp. 10–13). APACALL. https://www.apacall.org/research/books/7/

Canals, L. (2020). The effects of virtual exchanges on oral skills and motivation. *Language Learning & Technology, 24*(3), 103–119. https://doi.org/10125/44742

Cappellini, M., & Combe, C. (2022). Multiple online environments as complex systems: Toward an orchestration of environments. *Language Learning & Technology, 26*(1), 1–20. https://doi.org/10125/73497

Carillo, E. C. (2022). *MLA guide to digital literacy* (2nd ed.). Modern Language Association.

Carrier, M., Damerow, R. M., & Bailey, K. M. (Eds.). (2017). *Digital language learning and teaching: Research, theory, and practice*. Routledge.

Carrier, M., & Nye, A. (2017). Empowering teachers for the digital future. In M., Carrier, R. M. Damerow & K. M. Bailey (Eds.), *Digital language learning and teaching: Research, theory, and practice* (pp. 208–221). Routledge.

Chen, C. W.-Y. (2020). Analyzing online comments: A language-awareness approach to cultivating digital literacies. *Computer Assisted Language Learning, 33*(4), 435–454. https://doi.org/10.1080/09588221.2019.1569068

Çıraklı, M. Z., & Kılıçkaya, F. (2023). Integrating artificial intelligence into collaborative poetry. In J.-B. Son (Ed.), *Online language teaching in action* (pp. 70–73). APACALL. https://www.apacall.org/research/books/7/

Coiro, J. (2017). *Teaching adolescents how to evaluate the quality of online information*. Edutopia. https://www.edutopia.org/blog/evaluating-quality-of-online-info-julie-coiro

Comas-Quinn, A., de los Arcos, B., & Mardomingo, R. (2012). Virtual learning environments (VLEs) for distance language learning: Shifting tutor roles in a contested space for interaction. *Computer Assisted Language Learning, 25*(2), 129–143. https://doi.org/10.1080/09588221.2011.636055

Cote, T., & Milliner, B. (2018). A survey of EFL teachers' digital literacy: A report from a Japanese university. *Teaching English with Technology, 18*(4), 71–89. https://tewtjournal.org/download/6-a-survey-of-efl-teachers-digital-literacy-a-report-from-a-japanese-university-by-travis-cote-and-brett-milliner/

Coyle, Y., & Reverte Prieto, M. J. (2017). Children's interaction and lexical acquisition in text-based online chat. *Language Learning & Technology, 21*(2), 179–199. https://doi.org/10125/44617

Curwood, J. S. (2011). Teachers as learners: What makes technology-focused professional development effective? *English in Australia, 46*(3), 68–75.

Darvin, R. (2017) Language, ideology, and critical digital literacy. In S. L. Thorne & S. May (Eds.), *Language, education and technology* (3rd ed., pp. 17–30). Springer. https://doi.org/10.1007/978-3-319-02237-6_35

Darvin, R., & Hafner, C. A. (2022). Digital literacies in TESOL: Mapping out the terrain. *TESOL Quarterly, 56*(3), 865–882. https://doi.org/10.1002/tesq.3161

Dashtestani, S., & Hojatpanah, S. (2021). Digital literacy for Iranian EAP instructors: Challenges, opportunities, and current practices. *Foreign Language Research Journal, 11*(3), 417–433. https://doi.org/10.22059/JFLR.2021.330161.890

Dashtestani, R., & Hojatpanah, S. (2022). Digital literacy of EFL students in a junior high school in Iran: Voices of teachers, students and Ministry Directors. *Computer Assisted Language Learning, 35*(4), 635–665. https://doi.org/10.1080/09588221.2020.1744664

Deardorff, D. K. (2006). Identification and assessment of intercultural competence as a student outcome of internationalization. *Journal of Studies in International Education, 10*(3), 241–266. https://doi.org/10.1177/1028315306287002

Dodel, M. & Mesch, G. (2018). Inequality in digital skills and the adoption of online safety behaviors. *Information, Communication & Society, 21*(5), 712–728. https://doi.org/10.1080/1369118X.2018.1428652

Donaghy, K. (n.d.). *Keeping your learners safe online*. British Council. https://www.teachingenglish.org.uk/sites/teacheng/files/Online-safety.pdf

Dreamson, N. (2020). *Critical understandings of digital technology in education: Meta-connective pedagogy*. Routledge.

Dudeney, G., Hockly, N., & Pegrum, M. (2013). *Digital literacies*. Pearson Education.

eSafety Commissioner (2021). *Best practice framework for online safety education: Implementation guide*. Australian Government. https://www.esafety.gov.au/sites/default/files/2021-07/BPF%20-%20Implementation%20guide.pdf

Eshet-Alkalai, Y. (2004). Digital literacy: A conceptual framework for survival skills in the digital era. *Journal of Educational Multimedia and Hypermedia, 13*(1), 93–106. https://www.learntechlib.org/primary/p/4793/

European Commission. (2020). *Digital Education Action Plan 2021–2027*. European Commission. https://education.ec.europa.eu/focus-topics/digital-education/action-plan

Falloon, G. (2020). From digital literacy to digital competence: The teacher digital competency (TDC) framework. *Educational Technology Research and Development, 68*(5), 2449–2472. https://doi.org/10.1007/s11423-020-09767-4

Fantini, A. & Tirmizi, A. (2006). Exploring and assessing intercultural competence. *World Learning Publications, 1*. https://digitalcollections.sit.edu/worldlearning_publications/1/

Farrell, T. S. C. (2018). *Reflective language teaching: Practical applications for TESOL teachers* (2nd ed.). Bloomsbury Academic.

Fautley, M. & Savage, J. (2007). *Creativity in secondary education*. Learning Matters.

Ferrari, A. (2012). *Digital competence in practice: An analysis of frameworks*. European Commission. https://doi.org/10.2791/82116

Ferrari, A. (2013). *DIGCOMP: A framework for developing and understanding digital competence in Europe*. European Commission. https://publications.jrc.ec.europa.eu/repository/bitstream/JRC83167/lb-na-26035-enn.pdf

Fraga-Varela, F. & Alonso-Ferreiro, A. (2022). Digital competence in primary education and the limits of 1:1 computing. *Canadian Journal of Learning and Technology, 48*(2), 1–18. https://doi.org/10.21432/cjlt27955

Galla, C. K. (2016). Indigenous language revitalization, promotion, and education: Function of digital technology. *Computer Assisted Language Learning, 29*(7), 1137–1151. https://doi.org/10.1080/09588221.2016.1166137

Gardner, H. (1983). *Frames of mind: The theory of multiple intelligences*. Basic Books.

Gardner, H. (1999). *Intelligence reframed: Multiple intelligences for the 21st century*. Basic Books.

Gilster, P. (1997). *Digital literacy*. John Wiley & Sons.

Given, L. M. (2023, March 23). AI tools are generating convincing misinformation. Engaging with them means being on high alert. *The Conversation*. https://

theconversation.com/ai-tools-are-generating-convincing-misinformation-engaging-with-them-means-being-on-high-alert-202062

Gleason, B. & von Gillern, S. (2018). Digital citizenship with social media: Participatory practices of teaching and learning in secondary education. *Educational Technology & Society, 21*(1), 200–212. https://drive.google.com/file/d/1HrRqdSBpVoxSxRCoFJZFx0_7aQT16gTp/view

Godwin-Jones, R. (2015). Contributing, creating, curating: Digital literacies for language learners. *Language Learning & Technology, 19*(3), 8–20. https://doi.org/10125/44427

Godwin-Jones, R. (2016). Looking back and ahead: 20 years of technologies for language learning. *Language Learning & Technology, 20*(2), 5–12. https://doi.org/10125/44457

Göl, B., Özbek, U., & Horzum, M.B. (2023). Digital distraction levels of university students in emergency remote teaching. *Education and Information Technologies, 28*, 9149–9170. https://doi.org/10.1007/s10639-022-11570-y

Gruba, P. & Nguyen, N. B. C. (2019). Evaluating technology integration in a Vietnamese university language program. *Computer Assisted Language Learning, 32*(5–6), 619–637. https://doi.org/10.1080/09588221.2018.1527365

Gu, M. M., Huang, C. F., & Lee, C.-K. J. (2023). Investigating university students' digital citizenship development through the lens of digital literacy practice: A translingual and transemiotizing perspective. *Linguistics and Education, 77*, 101226. https://doi.org/10.1016/j.linged.2023.101226

Gui, M. & Argentin, G. (2011). Digital skills of internet natives: Different forms of digital literacy in a random sample of northern Italian high school students. *New Media & Society, 13*(6), 963–980. https://doi.org/10.1177/1461444810389751

Guikema, J. P. & Menke, M. R. (2014). Preparing future foreign language teachers: The role of digital literacies. In J. P. Guikema & L. Williams (Eds.), *Digital literacies in foreign and second language education* (pp. 265–285). CALICO.

Guikema, J. P. & Williams, L. (2014). Digital literacies from multiple perspectives. In J. P. Guikema & L. Williams (Eds.), *Digital literacies in foreign and second language education* (pp. 1–7). CALICO.

Hafner, C. A. (2014). Embedding digital literacies in English language teaching: Students' digital video projects as multimodal ensembles. *TESOL Quarterly, 48*(4), 655–685. https://doi.org/10.1002/tesq.138

Hafner, C. A., Chik, A., & Jones, R. H. (2015). Digital literacies and language learning. *Language Learning & Technology, 19*(3), 1–7. https://doi.org/10125/44426

Hague, C. & Payton, S. (2010). *Digital literacy across the curriculum: A Futurelab handbook*. Futurelab. https://www.nfer.ac.uk/publications/digital-literacy-across-the-curriculum/

Hammond (2017). Online collaboration and cooperation: The recurring importance of evidence, rationale and viability. *Education and Information Technologies, 22*, 1005–1024. https://doi.org/10.1007/s10639-016-9469-x

Hargittai, E. (2002). Second-level digital divide: Differences in people's online skills. *First Monday, 7*(4). https://doi.org/10.5210/fm.v7i4.942

Hartikainen, H., Iivari, N., & Kinnula, M. (2019). Children's design recommendations for online safety education. *International Journal of Child-Computer Interaction, 22*, 100146. https://doi.org/10.1016/j.ijcci.2019.100146

Hauck, M. (2019) Virtual exchange for (critical) digital literacy skills development. *European Journal of Language Policy, 11*(2), 187–210. https://doi.org/10.3828/ejlp.2019.12

Hauck, M. & Kurek, M. (2017) Digital literacies in teacher preparation. In S. L. Thorne & S. May (Eds.), *Language, education and technology* (3rd ed., pp. 275–287). Springer. https://doi.org/10.1007/978-3-319-02237-6_22

Hobbs, R. (2010). *Digital and media literacy: A plan of action*. The Aspen Institute. https://www.aspeninstitute.org/wp-content/uploads/2010/11/Digital_and_Media_Literacy.pdf

Hockly, N. (2015). Digital literacies. In G. Pickering & P. Gunashekar (Eds.), *Innovation in English language teacher education* (pp. 232–236). British Council. https://www.britishcouncil.in/sites/default/files/tec14_papers_final_online.pdf

Howell, J. & McMaster, N. (2022). *Teaching with technologies: Pedagogies for collaboration, communication, and creativity* (2nd ed.). Oxford University Press.

Hubbard, P. (2013). Making a case for learner training in technology enhanced language learning environments. *CALICO Journal, 30*(2), 163–178. https://doi.org/10.11139/cj.30.2.163-178

Hubbard, P. (2021). *An invitation to CALL: Foundations of computer-assisted language learning*. APACALL. https://www.apacall.org/research/books/6/

Hull, G. A. & Stornaiuolo, A. (2010). Literate arts in a global world: Reframing social networking as cosmopolitan practice. *Journal of Adolescent & Adult Literacy, 54*(2), 85–97. https://doi.org/10.1598/JAAL.54.2.1

Hung, S.-T. A. (2019). Creating digital stories: EFL learners' engagement, cognitive and metacognitive skills. *Educational Technology & Society, 22*(2), 26–37. https://drive.google.com/file/d/17hpl8cP7toTfRjPIK2McL-EzKxy6hLY4/view

Instefjord, E. J. & Munthe, E. (2017). Educating digitally competent teachers: A study of integration of professional digital competence in teacher education. *Teaching and Teacher Education, 67*, 37–45. https://doi.org/10.1016/j.tate.2017.05.016

ISTE (International Society for Technology in Education). (2017). *ISTE standards for educators*. ISTE. https://iste.org/standards/educators

Ivers, K. S., & Barron, A. E. (2015). *Digital content creation in schools: A common core approach*. ABC-CLIO.

Janssen, J., Stoyanov, S., Ferrari, A., Punie, Y., Pannekeet, K., & Sloep, P. (2013). Experts' views on digital competence: Commonalities and differences. *Computers & Education, 68*, 473–481. https://doi.org/10.1016/j.compedu.2013.06.008

Jenkins, H., Ito, M., & Boyd, D. (2016). *Participatory culture in a networked era: A conversation on youth, learning, commerce, and politics*. Polity Press.

Jin, H., Karatay, Y., Bordbarjavidi, F., Yang, J., Kochem, T., Muhammad, A. A., & Hegelheimer, V. (2022). Exploring global online course participants' interactions: Value of high-level engagement. *ReCALL, 34*(3), 291–308. https://doi.org/10.1017/S0958344021000331

Jisc. (2014). *Developing students' digital literacy*. https://digitalcapability.jiscinvolve.org/wp/files/2014/09/JISC_REPORT_Digital_Literacies_280714_PRINT.pdf

Jisc. (n.d.). *Building digital capability*. https://digitalcapability.jisc.ac.uk/

Jones, R. H. (2021). The text is reading you: Teaching language in the age of the algorithm. *Linguistics and Education, 62*, 100750. https://doi.org/10.1016/j.linged.2019.100750

Jones, R. H. & Hafner, C. A. (2021). *Understanding digital literacies: A practical introduction*. Routledge.

Jung, Y., Kim, Y., Lee, H., Cathey, R., Carver, J., & Skalicky, S. (2019). Learner perception of multimodal synchronous computer-mediated communication in foreign language classrooms. *Language Teaching Research, 23*(3), 287–309. https://doi.org/10.1177/1362168817731910

Kahveci, P. (2021). Language teachers' digital literacy and self-efficacy: Are they related? *ELT Research Journal, 10*(2), 123–139. https://dergipark.org.tr/en/pub/eltrj/issue/67200/819546

Kang, S. & Kim, Y. (2021). Examining the quality of mobile-assisted, video-making task outcomes: The role of proficiency, narrative ability, digital literacy, and motivation. *Language Teaching Research*. Advance online publication. https://doi.org/10.1177/13621688211047984

Karagul, B., Seker, M., & Aykut, C. (2021). Investigating students' digital literacy levels during online education due to COVID-19 pandemic. *Sustainability, 13*(21), 11878. https://doi.org/10.3390/su132111878

Katz, A. (2012). *Cyberbullying and e-safety: What educators and other professionals need to know*. Jessica Kingsley.

Kelly, S. M. (2023, February 9). The way we search for information online is about to change. *CNN Business*. https://edition.cnn.com/2023/02/09/tech/ai-search/index.html

Kern, R. (2015). *Language, literacy, and technology*. Cambridge University Press.

Kern, R. (2018). Five principles of a relational pedagogy: Integrating social, individual, and material dimensions of language use. *Journal of Technology and Chinese Language Teaching, 9*(2), 1–14. http://www.tclt.us/journal/2018v9n2/kern.pdf

Kern, R. (2021). Twenty-five years of digital literacies in CALL. *Language Learning & Technology, 25*(3), 132–150. https://doi.org/10125/73453

Kohnke, L., Moorhouse, B. L., & Zou, D. (2023). ChatGPT for language teaching and learning. *RELC Journal, 54*(2), 537–550. https://doi.org/10.1177/00336882231162868

Korisztek, R. (2021). *Teachers' digital literacy and implications when teaching online*. https://www.cambridge.org/elt/blog/2021/07/13/teachers-digital-literacy-teaching-online/

Kuiper, E. & Volman, M. (2008). The web as a source of information for students in K-12 education. In J. Coiro, M. Knobel, C. Lankshear & D. J. Leu (Eds.), *Handbook of research on new literacies* (pp. 241–246). Erlbaum.

Kurek, M. & Hauck, M. (2014). Closing the digital divide - A framework for multiliteracy training. In J. P. Guikema & L. Williams (Eds.), *Digital literacies in foreign and second language education* (pp. 119–140). CALICO.

Lankshear, C. & Knobel, M. (2006). Digital literacy and digital literacies: Policy, pedagogy and research considerations for education. *Nordic Journal of Digital Literacy, 1*(1), 12–24. https://doi.org/10.18261/ISSN1891-943X-2006-01-03

Lankshear, C. & Knobel, M. (2008). Introduction: Digital literacies – Concepts, policies and practices. In C. Lankshear & M. Knobel (Eds.), *Digital literacies: Concepts, policies and practices* (pp. 1–16). Peter Lang.

La Trobe University Digital Literacies Framework Reference Group. (2019). *Digital literacies framework*. https://www.latrobe.edu.au/__data/assets/pdf_file/0005/995963/digital-literacies-framework.pdf

Lee, J. S. (2019). Informal digital learning of English and second language vocabulary outcomes: Can quantity conquer quality? *British Journal of Educational Technology, 50*(2), 767–778. https://doi.org/10.1111/bjet.12599

Lee, J. S. (2022). *Informal digital learning of English: Research to practice*. Routledge.

Lenkaitis, C. A. (2022). Integrating the United Nations' sustainable development goals: Developing content for virtual exchanges. *Language Learning & Technology, 26*(1), 1–20. https://doi.org/10125/73470

Leu, D. J., Forzani, E., Rhoads, C., Maykel, C., Kennedy, C., & Timbrell, N. (2015). The new literacies of online research and comprehension: Rethinking the reading achievement gap. *Reading Research Quarterly, 50*(1), 37–59. https://doi.org/10.1002/rrq.85

Levak, N. & Son, J.-B. (2017). Facilitating second language learners' listening comprehension with Second Life and Skype. *ReCALL, 29*(2), 200–218. https://doi.org/10.1017/S0958344016000215

Li, R. (2022). Research trends of blended language learning: A bibliometric synthesis of SSCI-indexed journal articles during 2000-2019. *ReCALL, 34*(3), 309–326. https://doi.org/10.1017/S0958344021000343

Liaw, M.-L. (2019). EFL learners' intercultural communication in an open social virtual environment. *Educational Technology & Society, 22*(2), 38–55. https://drive.google.com/file/d/1n-VYyViAhcJKWySsaHApkYofrg5IkVxn/view

Liu, K.-P., Tai, S.-J. D., & Liu, C.-C. (2018). Enhancing language learning through creation: The effect of digital storytelling on student learning motivation and performance in a school English course. *Education Technology Research Development, 66*, 913–935. https://doi.org/10.1007/s11423-018-9592-z

Lonan, V. (2021). *Digital competence: What skills do you need to develop during the pandemic?* EU4Digital. https://eufordigital.eu/digital-competence-what-skills-do-you-need-to-develop-during-the-pandemic/

Lotherington, H. & Jenson, J. (2011). Teaching multimodal and digital literacy in L2 settings: New literacies, new basics, new pedagogies. *Annual Review of Applied Linguistics, 31*, 226–246. https://doi.org/10.1017/S0267190511000110

Lotherington, H. & Ronda, N. (2014). 2B or not 2B? From pencil to multimodal programming: New frontiers in communicative competencies. In J. P. Guikema & L. Williams (Eds.), *Digital literacies in foreign and second language education* (pp. 9–28). CALICO.

Lozano, A. A. & Izquierdo, J. (2019). The use of technology in second language education: Some considerations to overcome the digital divide. *Emergent Trends in Education, 2*(3), 52–70. https://doi.org/10.19136/etie.a2n3.3250

Mackenzie, A. & Makin, L. (2003). Beyond student instruction: Information skills for staff. *New Review of Academic Librarianship, 9*(1), 113–130. https://doi.org/10.1080/13614530410001692077

Manegre, M. & Sabiri, K. A. (2022). Online language learning using virtual classrooms: An analysis of teacher perceptions. *Computer Assisted Language Learning, 35*(5–6), 973–988. https://doi.org/10.1080/09588221.2020.1770290

Marín, V. I., Carpenter, J. P., Tur, G., & Williamson-Leadley, S. (2023). Social media and data privacy in education: An international comparative study of perceptions among pre-service teachers. *Journal of Computers in Education, 10*(4), 769–795. https://doi.org/10.1007/s40692-022-00243-x

Martin, A. (2005). DigEuLit – A European framework for digital literacy: A progress report. *Journal of eLiteracy, 2*, 130–136.

McLay, K. & Reyes, V. C. Jr. (2019). Identity and digital equity: Reflections on a university educational technology course. *Australasian Journal of Educational Technology, 35*(6), 15–29. https://doi.org/10.14742/ajet.5552

Meishar-Tal, H. (2015). Teachers' use of Wikipedia with their students. *Australian Journal of Teacher Education, 40*(12), 126–140. https://doi.org/10.14221/ajte.2015v40n12.9

Meniado, J. C. (2023). Digital language teaching 5.0: Technologies, trends and competencies. *RELC Journal, 54*(2), 461–473. https://doi.org/10.1177/00336882231160610

Meyers, E., Erickson, I., & Small, R. (2013). Digital literacy and informal learning environments: An introduction. *Learning, Media and Technology, 38*(4), 355–367. https://doi.org/10.1080/17439884.2013.783597

Milton, M. & Vozzo, L. (2013). Digital literacy and digital pedagogies for teaching literacy: Pre-service teachers' experience on teaching rounds. *Journal of Literacy and Technology, 14*(1), 72–97. http://www.literacyandtechnology.org/uploads/1/3/6/8/136889/jlt_v14_1_milton_vozzo.pdf

Mishra, P. & Koehler, M. (2006). Technological pedagogical content knowledge: A framework for teacher knowledge. *Teachers College Record, 108*(6), 1017–1054. https://doi.org/10.1111/j.1467-9620.2006.00684.x

Mizza, D. & Rubio, F. (2020). *Creating effective blended language learning courses: A research-based guide from planning to evaluation.* Cambridge University Press.

Mohammad, T., Hussin, N. A. M., & Husin, M. H. (2022). Online safety awareness and human factors: An application of the theory of human ecology. *Technology in Society, 68*, 101823. https://doi.org/10.1016/j.techsoc.2021.101823

Murray, L., Giralt, M., & Benini, S. (2020). Extending digital literacies: Proposing an agentive literacy to tackle the problems of distractive technologies in language learning. *ReCALL, 32*(3), 250–271. https://doi.org/10.1017/S0958344020000130

Mutta, M., Pelttari, S., Salmi, L., Chevalier, A., & Johansson, M. (2014). Digital literacy in academic language learning contexts: Developing information-seeking competence. In J. P. Guikema & L. Williams (Eds.), *Digital literacies in foreign and second language education* (pp. 227–244). CALICO.

National Council of Teachers of English. (2007). *21st-century literacies: A policy research brief.* NCTE. https://cdn.ncte.org/nctefiles/resources/positions/chron1107researchbrief.pdf

Ng, D. T. K., Leung, J. K. L., Su, J., Ng, R. C. W., & Chu, S. K. W. (2023). Teachers' AI digital competencies and twenty-first century skills in the post-pandemic world. *Education Technology Research and Development, 71*, 137–161. https://doi.org/10.1007/s11423-023-10203-6

Ng, W. (2012). Can we teach digital natives digital literacy? *Computers & Education, 59*, 1065–1078. https://doi.org/10.1016/j.compedu.2012.04.016

Nguyen, L. A. T., & Habók, A. (2022). Digital literacy of EFL students: An empirical study in Vietnamese universities. *LIBRI: International Journal of Libraries and Information Studies (Libri), 72*(1), 53–66. https://doi.org/10.1515/libri-2020-0165

Nicolaou, A. (2021). Technological mediation in a global competence virtual exchange project: A critical digital literacies perspective. In S. Papadima-Sophocleous, E. Kakoulli Constantinou & C. N. Giannikas (Eds.), *Tertiary education language learning: A collection of research* (pp. 111–131). Research-publishing.net. https://doi.org/10.14705/rpnet.2021.51.1257

O'Dowd, R. & Dooly, M. (2022). Exploring teachers' professional development through participation in virtual exchange. *ReCALL, 34*(1), 21–36. https://doi.org/10.1017/S0958344021000215

O'Dowd, R. & O'Rourke, B. (2019). New developments in virtual exchange in foreign language education. *Language Learning & Technology, 23*(3), 1–7. https://doi.org/10125/44690

Ortlieb, E., Susca, A., Votypka, J., & Cheek, E. H. Jr. (2018). Disruptive innovations for teacher education. In E. Ortlieb, E. H. Jr. Cheek & P. Semingson (Eds.), *Best practices in teaching digital literacies* (pp. 1–11). Emerald Publishing.

Oskoz, A. & Elora, I. (2014). Integrating digital stories in the writing class: Toward a 21st century literacy. In J. P. Guikema & L. Williams (Eds.), *Digital literacies in foreign and second language education* (pp. 179–200). CALICO.

Oskoz, A. & Elola, I. (2020). *Digital L2 writing literacies: Directions for classroom practice.* Equinox Publishing.

Payton, S. & Hague, C. (2010). *Digital literacy professional development resource*. Futurelab. https://www.nfer.ac.uk/publications/digital-literacy-professional-development-resource/

Pegrum, M. (2016). Languages and literacies for digital lives. In E. Martín-Monje, I. Elorza & B. G. Riaza (Eds.), *Technology-enhanced language learning for specialized domains: Practical applications and mobility* (pp. 9–22). Routledge.

Pegrum, M. (2023). *Digital literacies*. https://markpegrum.com/overview-of-digital-learning/digital-literacies/

Peters, M. & Frankoff, M. (2014). New literacy practices and plagiarism: A study of strategies for digital scrapbooking. In J. P. Guikema & L. Williams (Eds.), *Digital literacies in foreign and second language education* (pp. 245–264). CALICO.

Philpott, A., & Son, J.-B. (2022). Leaderboards in an EFL course: Student performance and motivation. *Computers & Education, 190*, 104605. https://doi.org/10.1016/j.compedu.2022.104605

Porat, E., Blau, I., & Barak, A. (2018). Measuring digital literacies: Junior high-school students' perceived competencies versus actual performance. *Computers & Education, 126*(2018), 23–36. https://doi.org/10.1016/j.compedu.2018.06.030

Price-Dennis, D., Holmes, K., & Smith, E. (2015). Exploring digital literacy practices in an inclusive classroom. *The Reading Teacher, 69*(2), 195–205. https://doi.org/10.1002/trtr.1398

Ragnedda, M. & Muschert, G. W. (Eds.). (2013). *The digital divide: The internet and social inequality in international perspective*. Routledge.

Redecker, C. (2017). *European framework for the digital competence of educators: DigCompEdu*. Joint Research Centre. https://publications.jrc.ec.europa.eu/repository/handle/JRC107466

Reinhardt, J., & Thorne, S. L. (2019). Digital literacies as emergent multifarious literacies. In N. Arnold & L. Ducate (Eds.), *Engaging language learners through CALL* (pp. 208–239). Equinox.

Ribble, M. (n.d.). *Nine elements: Nine themes of digital citizenship*. Retrieved August 1, 2023, from https://www.digitalcitizenship.net/nine-elements.html

Richards, J. C., & Lockhart, C. (1996). *Reflective teaching in second language classrooms*. Cambridge University Press.

Robinson, J., Dusenberry, L., Hutter, L., Lawrence, H., Frazee, A., & Burnett, R. E. (2019). State of the field: Teaching with digital tools in the writing and communication Classroom. *Computers and Composition, 54*, 102511. https://doi.org/10.1016/j.compcom.2019.102511

Rodríguez-de-Dios, I., & Igartua, J.-J. (2016). Skills of digital literacy to address the risks of interactive communication. *Journal of Information Technology Research, 9*(1), 54–64. https://doi.org/10.4018/JITR.2016010104

Romeo, K. & Hubbard, P. (2008). Pervasive CALL learner training for improving listening proficiency. *Proceedings of the WorldCALL 2008 Conference* (pp. 83–85). https://web.archive.org/web/20170706081046/http://www.j-let.org/~wcf/proceedings/d-060.pdf

Rouet, J.-F., Ros, C., Goumi, A., Macedo-Rouet, M., & Dinet, J. (2011). The influence of surface and deep cues on primary and secondary school students' assessment of relevance in web menus. *Learning and Instruction, 21*(2), 205–219. https://doi.org/10.1016/j.learninstruc.2010.02.007

Rowley, J. (2015). The changing nature of information behaviour. In M. Khosrow-Pour (Ed.), *Encyclopedia of information science and technology* (3rd ed.) (pp. 3955–3961). IGI Global.

Rowley, J. & Johnson, F. (2013). Understanding trust formation in digital information sources: The case of Wikipedia. *Journal of Information Science, 39*(4), 494–508. https://doi.org/10.1177/0165551513477820

Sanderson, M., Thomas, J., Hegarty, K., & Given, L. M. (2023, September 4). Google turns 25: The search engine revolutionised how we access information, but will it survive AI? *The Conversation.* https://theconversation.com/google-turns-25-the-search-engine-revolutionised-how-we-access-information-but-will-it-survive-ai-212367

Santosa, M. H., & Ivone, F. M. (2020). Virtual reality-infused language learning. In J.-B. Son (Ed.), *Technology-enhanced language teaching in action* (pp. 75–78). APACALL. https://www.apacall.org/research/books/5/

Santoveña-Casal, S. & López, S. R. (2023). Mapping of digital pedagogies in higher education. *Education and Information Technologies.* Advance online publication. https://doi.org/10.1007/s10639-023-11888-1

Sato, T., Murase, F., & Burden, T. (2020). An empirical study on vocabulary recall and learner autonomy through mobileassisted language learning in blended learning settings. *CALICO Journal, 37*(3), 254–276. https://doi.org/10.1558/cj.40436

Seghayer, K. A. (2020). Investigating the adequacy of EFL learners' L2 digital literacy skills, consistency of self-assessed competence, and actual performance. *International Journal of Computer-Assisted Language Learning, 10*(2), 1–22. https://doi.org/10.4018/IJCALLT.2020040101

Shillair, R., Cotten, S. R., Tsai, H.-Y. S., Alhabash, S., LaRose, R., & Rifon, N. J. (2015). Online safety begins with you and me: Convincing internet users to protect themselves. *Computers in Human Behavior, 48*, 199–207. https://doi.org/10.1016/j.chb.2015.01.046

Shin, S.-K. (2015). Teaching critical, ethical, and safe use of ICT in pre-service teacher education. *Language Learning & Technology, 19*(1), 181–197. https://doi.org/10125/44408

Shoecraft, K. (2023). Technology enhanced learning: Applying Padlet, VoiceThread and Microsoft Teams in online university courses. *TESOL in Context, 31*(2), 69–94. https://ojs.deakin.edu.au/index.php/tesol/article/view/1861/1590

Singer, G., Norbisrath, U., & Lewandowski, D. (2013). Ordinary search engine users carrying out complex search tasks. *Journal of Information Science, 39*(3), 346–358. https://doi.org/10.1177/0165551512466974

Son, J.-B. (2002). Online discussion in a CALL course for distance language teachers. *CALICO Journal, 20*(1), 127–144. https://journal.equinoxpub.com/Calico/article/view/998

Son, J.-B. (2006). Using online discussion groups in a CALL teacher training course. *RELC Journal, 37*(1), 123–135. https://doi.org/10.1177/0033688206063478

Son, J.-B. (2010). *Online tools for language teaching.* https://drjbson.com/projects/tools/

Son, J.-B. (2014a). Moving beyond basics: From CALL coursework to classroom practice and professional development. In J.-B. Son (Ed.), *Computer-assisted language learning: Learners, teachers and tools* (pp. 122–149). Cambridge Scholars Publishing.

Son, J.-B. (2014b). Learning about computer-assisted language learning: Online tools and professional development. In J.-B. Son (Ed.), *Computer-assisted language learning: Learners, teachers and tools* (pp. 173–186). Cambridge Scholars Publishing.

Son, J.-B. (2015). *Digital literacy.* https://drjbson.com/projects/dl/

Son, J.-B. (2016). Selecting and evaluating mobile apps for language learning. In A. Palalas & M. Ally (Eds.), *The international handbook of mobile-assisted language learning* (pp. 161–179). China Central Radio & TV University Press. https://drjbson.com/papers/MALL_Ch6_JS_2016.pdf

Son, J.-B. (2017). *Online activities for language learning.* https://drjbson.com/projects/oall/

Son, J.-B. (2018). *Teacher development in technology-enhanced language teaching.* Palgrave Macmillan. https://doi.org/10.1007/978-3-319-75711-7

Son, J.-B. (2019). Learner training in digital language learning for pre-service translators and interpreters. In J.-B. Son (Ed.), *Context-specific computer-assisted language learning: Research, development and practice* (pp. 27–49). APACALL. https://www.apacall.org/research/books/4/

Son, J.-B. (Ed.). (2020a). *Technology-enhanced language teaching in action.* APACALL. https://www.apacall.org/research/books/5/

Son, J.-B. (2020b). Digital language teaching and teacher development. In J.-B. Son (Ed.), *Technology-enhanced language teaching in action* (pp. 3–13). APACALL. https://www.apacall.org/research/books/5/

Son, J.-B. (2020c). Mobile-assisted academic vocabulary learning. In J.-B. Son (Ed.), *Technology-enhanced language teaching in action* (pp. 18–21). APACALL. https://www.apacall.org/research/books/5/

Son, J.-B. (2021, December). Technology standards for teachers and professional development frameworks. *APACALL Newsletter, 25*, 6–12. https://www.apacall.org/news/APACALL_Newsletter25.pdf

Son, J.-B. (Ed.). (2023a). *Online language teaching in action.* APACALL. https://www.apacall.org/research/books/7/

Son, J.-B. (2023b). Tracking understanding and learning in videoconferencing. In J.-B. Son (Ed.), *Online language teaching in action* (pp. 3–5). APACALL. https://www.apacall.org/research/books/7/

Son, J.-B. (2023c). *Online tools for language teaching 2023*. https://drjbson.com/projects/tools/index2.html

Son, J.-B. (2023d). *Online activities for language learning 2023*. https://drjbson.com/projects/oall/index2.html

Son, J.-B., Park, S.-S., & Park, M. (2017). Digital literacy of language learners in two different contexts. *The JALT CALL Journal, 13*(2), 77–96. https://doi.org/10.29140/jaltcall.v13n2.213

Son, J.-B., Robb, T., & Charismiadji, I. (2011). Computer literacy and competency: A survey of Indonesian teachers of English as a foreign language. *CALL-EJ, 12*(1), 26–42. http://callej.org/journal/12-1/Son_2011.pdf

Son, J.-B., Ružić, N. K., & Philpott, A. (2023). Artificial intelligence technologies and applications for language learning and teaching. *Journal of China Computer-Assisted Language Learning*. Advance online publication. https://doi.org/10.1515/jccall-2023-0015

Stickler, U. (2022). *Technology and language teaching*. Cambridge University Press.

Stockwell, G. (2015). Digital media literacy in language teaching. *Journal of Korean Language Education, 36*, 361–381. https://doi.org/10.17313/jkorle.2015..36.361

Stockwell, G. (2022). *Mobile assisted language learning: Concepts, contexts and challenges*. Cambridge University Press.

Su, F. & Zou, D. (2022). Technology-enhanced collaborative language learning: Theoretical foundations, technologies, and implications. *Computer Assisted Language Learning, 35*(8), 1754–1788. https://doi.org/10.1080/09588221.2020.1831545

Tate, T. & Warschauer, M. (2017). The digital divide in language and literacy education. In S. Thorne & S. May (Eds.), *Language, education and technology* (pp. 45–56). Springer. https://doi.org/10.1007/978-3-319-02237-6_5

Taylor, M., Fudge, A., Mirriahi, N., & de Laat M. (2021). *Use of digital technology in education: Literature review*. Centre for Change and Complexity in Learning. https://www.education.sa.gov.au/docs/ict/digital-strategy-microsite/c31-digital-technologies-in-education-literature-review.pdf

TESOL (Teachers of English to Speakers of Other Languages). (2008). *TESOL technology standards framework*. TESOL.

The Centre for Social Justice. (2017). *Social justice in the digital age*. https://www.centreforsocialjustice.org.uk/wp-content/uploads/2018/03/CSJ_Digial_inclusion.pdf

Thorne, S. L. (2013). Digital literacies. In M. R. Hawkins (Ed.), *Framing languages and literacies: Socially situated views and perspectives* (pp. 192–218). Routledge.

Tinmaz, H., Lee, Y.-T., Fanea-Ivanovici, M., & Baber, H. (2022). A systematic review on digital literacy. *Smart Learning Environments, 9*(21), 1–18. https://doi.org/10.1186/s40561-022-00204-y

Tour, E. (2015). Digital mindsets: Teachers' technology use in personal life and teaching. *Language Learning & Technology, 19*(3), 124–139. https://doi.org/10125/44437

van Laar, E., van Deursen, A. J., van Dijk, J. A., & de Haan, J. (2017). The relation between 21st-century skills and digital skills: A systematic literature review. *Computers in Human Behavior, 72*, 577–588. https://doi.org/10.1016/j.chb.2017.03.010

Vartiainen, H., Pellas, L., Kahila, J., Valtonen, T., & Tedre, M. (2022). Pre-service teachers' insights on data agency. *New Media & Society*. Advance online publication. https://doi.org/10.1177/14614448221079626

Vuorikari, R., Kluzer, S., & Punie, Y. (2022). *DigComp 2.2: The digital competence framework for citizens*. Joint Research Centre, European Commission. https://doi.org/10.2760/115376

Waemusa, Z. & Jongwattanapaiboon, A. (2023). Divergence of everyday practices and school policy on mobile use: Challenges to developing EFL learners' digital literacies. *International Journal of Technology in Education, 6*(1), 37–48. https://doi.org/10.46328/ijte.294

Walsh, K., Pink, E., Ayling N., Sondergeld, A., Dallaston, E., Tournas, P., Serry, E., Trotter, S., Spanos, T., & Rogic, N. (2022). Best practice framework for online safety education: Results from a rapid review of the international literature, expert review, and stakeholder consultation. *International Journal of Child-Computer Interaction, 33*, 100474. https://doi.org/10.1016/j.ijcci.2022.100474

Wang, L., Chen, H. C., Lee, J. C.-K., Yu, E. K. W., & Tian, J. X. (2022). Investigation of technology-enhanced language learning and teaching e-resources/tools in the online context. *International Journal of Computer-Assisted Language Learning, 12*(1), 1–21. https://doi.org/10.4018/IJCALLT.307150

Ware, P., Kern, R., & Warschauer, M. (2016). The development of digital literacies. In R. M. Manchón & P. K. Matsuda (Eds.), *Handbook of second and foreign language writing* (pp. 307–328). De Gruyter. https://doi.org/10.1515/9781614511335-017

Warnecke, S. & Lominé, L. (2011). Planning and preparing for synchronous online teaching. In M. Nicolson, L. Murphy & M. Southgate (Eds.), *Language teaching in blended contexts* (pp. 126–139). Dunedin Academic Press.

Warner, C. & Dupuy, B. (2018). Moving toward multiliteracies in foreign language teaching: Past and present perspectives ... and beyond. *Foreign Language Annals, 51*(1), 116–128. https://doi.org/10.1111/flan.12316

Wilden, S. (2013, October). *The role of online tools in teacher development*. Talk at the first joint online conference of TESOL CALL-IS and IATEFL LTSIG.

Williams, L., Abraham, L. B., & Bostelmann, E. D. (2014). A survey-driven study of the use of digital tools for language learning and teaching. In J. P. Guikema & L. Williams (Eds.), *Digital literacies in foreign and second language education* (pp. 29–67). CALICO.

Wishart, J. M., Oades, C. E., & Morris, M. (2007). Using online role play to teach internet safety awareness. *Computers & Education, 48*(3), 460–473. https://doi.org/10.1016/j.compedu.2005.03.003

Wong, K. M. & Moorhouse, B. L. (2021). Digital competence and online language teaching: Hong Kong language teacher practices in primary and secondary classrooms. *System, 103*, 102653. https://doi.org/10.1016/j.system.2021.102653

Wongsa, M. & Son, J.-B. (2022). Enhancing Thai secondary school students' English speaking skills, attitudes and motivation with drama-based activities and Facebook. *Innovation in Language Learning and Teaching, 16*(1), 41–52. https://doi.org/10.1080/17501229.2020.1853134

Wu, Z. (2020). Tracing EFL writers' digital literacy practices in asynchronous communication: A multiple-case study. *Journal of Second Language Writing, 50*, 100754. https://doi.org/10.1016/j.jslw.2020.100754

Yaari, E., Baruchson-Arbib, S., & Bar-Ilan, J. (2011). Information quality assessment of community generated content: A user study of Wikipedia. *Journal of Information Science, 37*(5), 487–498. https://doi.org/10.1177/0165551511416065

Yeh, E. & Swinehart, N. (2022). Social media literacy in L2 environments: Navigating anonymous user-generated content. *Computer Assisted Language Learning, 35*(8), 1731–1753. https://doi.org/10.1080/09588221.2020.1830805

Young, A. & Son, J.-B. (2023). Synchronous computer-mediated communication and task-based learning in the EFL classroom. *Language Teaching Research*. Advance online publication. https://doi.org/10.1177/13621688231191309

Yu, B. & Zadorozhnyy, A. (2022). Developing students' linguistic and digital literacy skills through the use of multimedia presentations. *ReCALL, 34*(1), 95–109. https://doi.org/10.1017/S0958344021000136

Yuan, C., Wang, L., & Eagle, J. (2019). Empowering English language learners through digital literacies: Research, complexities, and implications. *Media and Communication, 7*(2), 128–136. https://doi.org/10.17645/mac.v7i2.1912

Zhang, Y., & Liu, G. L. (2023). Examining the impacts of learner backgrounds, proficiency level, and the use of digital devices on informal digital learning of English: An explanatory mixed-method study. *Computer Assisted Language Learning*. Advance online publication. https://doi.org/10.1080/09588221.2023.2267627

Zhang, Z., & Hyland, K. (2023). The role of digital literacy in student engagement with automated writing evaluation (AWE) feedback on second language writing. *Computer Assisted Language Learning*. Advance online publication. https://doi.org/10.1080/09588221.2023.2256815

Zoch, M., Myers, J., & Belcher, J. (2017). Teachers' engagement with new literacies: Support for implementing technology in the English/language arts classroom. *Contemporary Issues in Technology & Teacher Education, 17*(1), 25–52. https://citejournal.org/volume-17/issue-1-17/english-language-arts/teachers-engagement-with-new-literacies-support-for-implementing-technology-in-the-englishlanguage-arts-classroom

Zou, D., Huang, Y., & Xie, H. (2021). Digital game-based vocabulary learning: Where are we and where are we going? *Computer Assisted Language Learning, 34*(5–6), 751–777. https://doi.org/10.1080/09588221.2019.1640745

Index

Approach, 12, 14–16, 26, 37, 56, 63, 74, 81, 88, 90–91, 106–107, 112, 114, 125, 135, 140
AI (artificial intelligence), 16–17, 19–22, 82–86, 106, 140
Artificial intelligence, see AI
Assessment, 14, 17, 19, 26, 35, 38, 45, 53–54, 90, 104–106, 125, 131–132, 134, 136
Attitude, 1–4, 20, 22, 52, 55, 69–70, 111, 117, 125, 134

Blended learning, 12, 112, 135
Blog, 26, 33–34, 38–40, 51, 53, 70, 73, 75–76, 79–80, 92, 110–111, 116–117, 119, 123

CALL (computer-assisted language learning), 12, 14–15, 22, 52, 136
Classroom, 8–9, 12, 14, 19, 37, 39, 50, 52, 55–56, 62, 67, 69–70, 80, 86, 92–93, 96, 100, 102, 107, 112–113, 118, 120, 128–129, 132, 135–137, 143
CMC (computer-mediated communication), 12, 51–52, 65, 71, 91, 116, 136
Collaboration, 1, 3–8, 12–13, 17, 29, 46, 53, 55, 68–72, 74, 78–79, 82, 86–87, 94, 114, 117, 124, 127, 131–132, 134–136, 139
Communication, 1–8, 12–13, 17, 34, 46, 51–58, 61–63, 65–68, 70–71, 77, 81, 87, 91–92, 94–95, 105, 111–114, 117–118, 124, 127, 131–132, 135–138

Community, 2, 5, 13, 53–54, 56, 60, 64, 68–71, 91, 95, 99, 108, 113, 116, 118, 127, 134–136, 140
Computer-assisted language learning, see CALL
Computer-mediated communication, see CMC
Creation, 3, 5–7, 34–36, 38–43, 45–47, 49–50, 59, 69–70, 74, 78, 84, 87, 94, 97, 105, 117, 120, 123, 127, 131–132, 135
Critical thinking, 4–6, 23, 26, 29, 31, 34, 46, 83
Culture, 4, 31, 38, 52, 55, 70, 89, 91, 95, 114, 135, 141

Design, 8, 17, 22–23, 28, 30, 33–36, 39, 42, 45, 47, 52, 56, 58–59, 61, 64, 71, 74, 75, 82, 89, 94, 96, 99, 106–107, 111, 113, 115, 119, 125–126, 129, 133–136, 140, 142, 144
Digital
 age, 18, 88, 105
 capability, 3, 134
 channel, 53, 69
 citizenship, 55, 94–95, 99–100, 106
 competence, 2–3, 6, 14, 17, 34, 38, 53–54, 70, 90, 104–105, 131–134, 140
 content, 20, 34–38, 49–50, 70, 132
 context, 27, 34, 139
 data, 16, 95
 device, 5, 8–9, 11, 14, 16, 19, 24, 34, 94, 108–109, 112, 132
 distraction, 16, 18
 divide, 14, 18

161

Digital *(continued)*
  environment, 1, 13, 15, 18–19, 33–34, 50–51, 55, 67, 69, 87–88, 103, 107, 112, 116, 131–133, 139–140
  footprint, 96–97, 102
  format, 34, 37, 51, 74, 135
  identity, 3, 53, 90, 95
  life, 8, 100
  literacy, 1–2, 4–8, 12–20, 23–24, 32, 34, 37, 51–52, 54–55, 69–71, 74, 88–89, 92, 95, 103–108, 112, 114–117, 123, 126, 131, 134, 140, 143–144
  language learning, 15, 27, 102, 126, 131, 144
  language teaching, 103, 111, 116, 131, 134–135, 140, 144
  media, 3, 5, 24, 59, 70, 90
  network, 5, 51, 70
  pedagogy, 103, 108, 111–112, 131
  platform, 60, 114
  portfolio, 41–42, 131
  presentation, 11, 34
  proficiency, 3, 117
  resource, 1, 20, 70, 114, 131–132
  safety, 90, 92
  security, 88, 94
  skill, 3–4, 7, 14, 105, 108, 112–113
  society, 3, 5
  space, 19, 24, 86, 94
  storytelling, 37, 59
  teaching strategies, 103, 116
  technology, 1–3, 5, 8, 12, 14–16, 19, 35, 37, 51–52, 55, 67–71, 86–88, 103–105, 107–108, 111, 116, 131–136, 139, 142
  tool, 1–2, 12–13, 18, 23, 27, 35, 37–38, 45, 55–56, 59–60, 67, 71, 74–77, 95, 103–104, 112–115, 117, 123, 128, 130–131, 134–138, 140–141, 143–144
  wellbeing, 3, 90
  world, 1, 87, 94–95, 135

Evaluation, 5–7, 12, 14, 17, 19–20, 24–31, 33, 81, 89, 100, 105, 123, 140–141
Exploration, 1, 7, 13, 17, 23, 71, 76, 98, 116, 127, 135–136, 138

Feedback, 12, 27, 28, 31–32, 38–42, 44–45, 54, 59, 66, 70, 72–73, 75–78, 97–98, 100, 103, 106, 116, 125, 132, 134–135, 142

Game, 9–10, 12–13, 29, 32, 36, 62, 78, 89, 110, 120, 129
Grammar, 12, 28, 39, 41, 43, 57, 79, 113, 141

ICT (information and communication technology), 3–4, 7, 68
Implementation, 14–15, 54–55, 61, 129, 135
Information and communication technology, see ICT
Information search, 5, 7, 19–20, 22–23, 26–28, 33, 87, 123
Instruction, 15, 27, 40, 45, 58, 64, 76–78, 82, 84, 94, 100, 105–107, 114, 117, 131, 133
Interaction, 8, 12, 17, 35, 45–46, 51–53, 55–56, 66, 68–69, 71, 75, 78, 93–94, 116–117, 132–133, 136, 138
Intercultural understanding, 12–13, 39, 68
Internet, 9, 11, 19, 21, 23, 25–26, 83, 87–88, 93, 96–97, 107, 122

Language
  education, 12, 18, 70, 87, 112
  learner, 1, 12–13, 17, 20, 24, 27–28, 34, 38–39, 51, 55–56, 62–65, 68, 70, 87, 90–93, 102–105, 108, 112, 117, 123, 143

Index

lesson, 39, 41, 74, 89, 93, 102, 131, 144
skill, 23, 27–31, 34, 39–43, 47, 54, 57–61, 63, 65, 72, 74–75, 77–79, 83, 96–99, 117, 126, 128, 131
teacher, 1, 8, 12, 15, 17–18, 34, 38–39, 52, 62, 67, 71, 86, 90–93, 102–105, 107–108, 112, 115–117, 131, 134–136, 138, 140, 144
Learner training, 15, 56, 104, 128–130
Listening, 5, 9, 11, 23, 29–31, 40, 42, 58–61, 69, 72, 74, 77–80, 96, 98–99, 117, 131, 141

MALL (mobile-assisted language learning), 2, 128–129
Management, 3–4, 7, 10, 56, 71, 95, 111, 114, 117–118, 120, 122, 135
Mobile-assisted language learning, see MALL
Multimedia, 24, 31, 35–36, 52, 54, 58–60, 75, 142

Online
activity, 33, 61, 105, 127–129
safety, 5, 7, 87–89, 92–93, 96–99, 102, 124
tool, 22, 30, 47, 56, 62, 117–118, 127–129

Professional development, 10, 15, 22, 105, 115, 131–132, 134–135, 140
Pronunciation, 72, 79, 121, 141

Reading, 5, 9, 13, 23, 25, 28–31, 39, 41–42, 46, 49, 57, 59–60, 62, 66, 73–74, 78–80, 82, 85, 96–97, 99, 108, 128–129, 131, 141
Reflection, 1, 8–11, 13, 15, 18, 71, 88, 115–116, 127, 134–136, 139
Research, 8, 10–11, 20, 23–24, 27, 30–31, 36, 43–44, 47–48, 63, 65, 71, 75, 92, 104, 107, 114, 129, 134

Social
media, 9, 11, 13–14, 16, 21, 24, 33, 38, 51, 54–55, 70, 89, 95, 99, 115
network, 4, 23, 34, 38, 51, 53, 95–96, 108, 111–112, 116–118, 127
Speaking, 5, 29–31, 40, 42, 58–61, 72, 74, 77–80, 83, 96, 98–99, 117, 122, 131, 141

Teacher
development, 15, 17, 67, 71, 86, 135–136, 138
education, 14–16, 89, 105, 114, 134, 140
educator, 136, 140
training, 15, 52
Technology-enhanced language teaching, see TELT
Technology integration, 105, 131, 140
TELT (technology-enhanced language teaching), 135, 137

Virtual
exchange, 12–13, 15, 70, 115
reality, 43, 55
wall, 74, 76–77, 96–97, 99–100, 122
world, 72–73, 111, 117–118
Vocabulary, 28, 39, 41, 43, 56–57, 64, 73, 80–81, 113, 121, 128–129, 141

Wiki, 33, 38, 40, 43, 68–70, 74–76, 107, 110–111, 116–117, 119, 127, 134
Writing, 5, 8–9, 12, 14, 17, 23, 28–31, 39–42, 46–48, 57, 59–60, 73–76, 78–80, 82–85, 96–97, 99, 112–114, 116, 131, 141

www.ingramcontent.com/pod-product-compliance
Lightning Source LLC
Chambersburg PA
CBHW051542230426
43669CB00015B/2692